SEEKING SOLACE

SEEKING SOLACE

WiLd cAt iN a PrEsSuRe cOoKeR

ZAE RANKIN

Copyright © 2023 by Zae Rankin.

ISBN:	Softcover	979-8-3694-0580-2
	eBook	979-8-3694-0579-6

All rights reserved. No part of this book may be reproduced or transmitted in any form or by any means, electronic or mechanical, including photocopying, recording, or by any information storage and retrieval system, without permission in writing from the copyright owner.

Any people depicted in stock imagery provided by Getty Images are models, and such images are being used for illustrative purposes only.
Certain stock imagery © Getty Images.

Print information available on the last page.

Rev. date: 09/06/2023

To order additional copies of this book, contact:
Xlibris
844-714-8691
www.Xlibris.com
Orders@Xlibris.com
551842

CONTENTS

Author's Note vii
Prologue: When Friendship Terror Strikes xi

Chapter 1   Early Childhood Dynamics 1
Chapter 2   Summertimes On The Double Horseshoe Ranch 7
Chapter 3   Dances With Medication Cocktails 15
Chapter 4   A Hard Head Makes A Sore Butt 21
Chapter 5   Higher Education And Adventure Abroad 25
Chapter 6   And The Double Beat Goes On 50
Chapter 7   Marriage Merry-Go Round 59
Chapter 8   Hit And Run Crime Unsolved 77
Chapter 9   Aftermath And The Pains From Hell 91
Chapter 10 Fighting For Lasting Redemption 107
Chapter 11 Big Hope Arrives On Four Legs – Solas 112
Chapter 12 Solas' Final Days And His Dynamic Replacement 128

Epilogue: Ten Collaborator Questions 151

AUTHOR'S NOTE

Writing this memoir was like watching myself as a private detective searching back to the past for significant clues and leads to help solve a crime that had gone cold much too long. As a preteen accustomed to participating in creative activities, I had developed a love for writing fiction stories straight from my imagination. Even that activity was a mystery because how was I able to conceive my characters and the plots and circumstances I had them face?

In contrast to those days as a young writer of fiction storytelling, my medical emergency challenges, my treatments, my seeking emotional and mental stability, my suffering from heartbreaks caused by an abusive husband and abusive lovers, and my fighting the demons caused by drug and alcohol abuse – are all true and covers a six-decade period.

Furthermore, you will discover how my fortitude helped me to survive through my own periods of madness, and how I, at last, triumphed over the destructive behavior of strangers, acquaintances, and friends who wrestled with their own vicious addictions.

What's in a fictional replacement author name like ZAE RANKIN, and why? I had asked myself that question many times before I decided that the-out-of-the-blue "Zae" would represent my first birth name. With its simplistic spelling, the sound of her name intrigued me. My ancestral roots are a mixture of English, Irish, and Scottish. The surname Rankin is rooted in that mixture stemming from my great grandmother's side of the family. For the protection of innocent/guilty family members, friends, acquaintances, and strangers I've befriended, I had decided that a fictional namesake was needed. The names of other real people were exchanged for fictional ones.

In conclusion, the future title of the mystery crime drama *Harvest of the Ancestors* could be interchangeable with the title I have chosen for my memoir. I asked for an explanation from my writer friend-collaborator Raymond Cornelius Alexander.

"Why that particular title for your book, Raymond?"

"I hope this makes sense to you. Think of seeds and what they are designed to accomplish."

"Right. But some don't mature to produce what's intended."

"Definitely. Still, human genes/traits/other DNA factors repeat themselves throughout generations of future humans in the same family tree. A family member could acquire one or many of the following physiological characteristics: eye color and shape, hair color and texture, nose shape, body build. Included are strengths-weaknesses of hereditary diseases and other afflictions. Let's not discount super-abilities. The same goes for talents, whether "natural" or to be "discovered" through much trial and error practice." He smiled. "Imagine an adult clan of eight family members and each one is a high-powered defense attorney. What does that tell you? Not a coincidence. The so-called smart gene wins. See?"

"Seems so." I returned his smile.

I respected his definition and I hope you will discover for yourself that *seeds of harvest* were developed within me before and after I was born on January 30, 1962. (In October of that year, the Cuban Missile Crisis, overshadowed by US and Soviet Union tensions, would bring the world closer to nuclear war.)

Those early hereditary seeds survived my teen years, my young adult years, and then the much later years approaching my 60s. The unraveling of this memoir will expose a key, revolving door segment of my life, with the sincere hope that you, too, will appreciate how heredity helped me triumph as a multiple survivor of harrowing circumstances – medically, emotionally, mentally, chemically. Otherwise, you would not discover yet another determined woman who re-learned her life's lessons and the importance of adhering to life skills. A lesser-equipped human might have succumbed sooner.

SEEKING SOLACE: A MEMOIR boils down to my ancestral traits. My unscientific mind has discovered, amongst others, four: sustaining mental focus, when sober, persistence in accomplishing goals, resilience in face of repeat adversity, genuine empathy for particular animals. I still wonder if I was pre-destined to have more than a few chances to escape a tragic death. What would the world look like if each of us had nine lives to experiment with? And why, as an odds beater, am I still alive? *Miracle* is the best way I can describe it.

PROLOGUE

WHEN FRIENDSHIP TERROR STRIKES

Like a schoolyard bully knowing she can dominate a weak willed classmate, my alcoholic cravings dominated over my common sense and hunger to live an alcohol-free life. I had survived many rock bottom alcoholic episodes; one of those should have been enough. Yet, I was determined to assert myself into a larger web of negative, harmful circumstances and consequences.

I remember the day my warped brain faced a Hollywood-style splatter effect scene in the guest bedroom of a friend's apartment. On that rainy, depressing Saturday evening, my addiction was an insatiable monster again and I was broker than a welfare recipient mother of four down to her last slice of white bread. I was without other immediate resources to quell my alcoholic pangs. My friend Johnny Rahwaye wasn't going to sacrifice one penny; a $15 loan to buy even a cheap bottle of booze was out of the question. I couldn't thwart what had transformed itself into a godlike entity of liquid. The more for me, the better. That's how pernicious my appetite for the stuff had grown.

Johnny was expected to return home by six. My aggravating thirst conquered my fears, thereby allowing me to become a ghetto snoop dog in his master bedroom – a for-real garbage pit. He was a sloppy housekeeper who didn't give a damn about other people's negative impressions of him. Stale smelling fast food bags and grease-soiled wrappers. Mounds of smelly dirty clothes littered the old and faded shag carpet that hadn't been pampered by a thorough shampooing in years. The bed was a tornado aftermath and smelled musky, along with the offensive smell of stale cigarette butts languishing in an ashtray. He was a chronic chain smoker.

I wanted to pinch my nostrils but my passion to drink alcohol was top priority. I was hoping to discover cash in a security hideout. First, I lifted the foot of the king size mattress… no cash awaited to be "borrowed". I checked the head of the mattress… same empty results. Dang. Pissed me off and further aggravated my need of alcohol; soon wasn't even fast enough for me.

A scarred oak dresser adjacent to the left side of a walk-in closet was my next target. Like a clumsy burglar, my trembling fingers opened the first drawer and carefully snooped through its contents. I found no cash. Got the same results for the other three drawers. Then I snooped through small containers on top the dresser: condom box, pencil/ink pen canister, New Testament Bible, empty toothpaste container. More disappointment. More heartache all the way down to my abused liver.

My little alter ego voice shouted big time in my head: CHECK INSIDE THE MESSY CLOSET, YOU FOOL!

The top shelf was lined with half a dozen fancy colored boxes featuring Nike athletic shoes with sticker shock prices. The first box was empty. The next to last box contained a virgin pair. The final box felt heavy in a different way when I slid it toward me; that's when I realized I had discovered his surrogate piggy bank of coins… maybe $50 max.

My heart boom-*boomed!* A wave of sour sweat dispersed from my forehead to my chest. Would crazy Johnny suspect I had "borrowed" only $20? I wasn't a genuine thief – thankfully, not a hereditary trait in me. I foresaw paying him back his nickels, dimes, and quarters.

Oh goodness gracious! I could taste the liquor already racing through my blood and spreading over me multiple sensations sex couldn't match at times.

On foot, I rushed to a liquor store located five blocks from a traffic-congested intersection with a reputation for motorists killing pedestrians. Then I rushed back faster with a fifth of Russian Vodka.

It was close to 6 pm – Johnny Rahwaye's expected arrival– when I marched upstairs. My perennial false hope was sealed in another booze bottle.

I was cozy naked on the guest room bed. My straight sips bathed familiar sweet spots. But would only one fifth help me survive the night? Sure was counting on that outcome because I didn't dare raid Johnny's coin stash again. He was a temperamental, grumpy wolf of a bastard who lacked patience and his logic about life in general was far flung into the universe.

He was no typical dummy, though. To this day, I still don't know exactly how he found out about the tampering of his coin-filled shoebox several hours later.

He knew I was broke, didn't have enough cash to purchase even a candy bar. I had already hidden the remaining Vodka in my puffy hooded winter coat. He would have no reason to check its left sleeve.

As a safety precaution, I crammed two sticks of spearmint chewing gum into my mouth. Chewed like an annoyed cow to get the ingredients to disperse sooner. I then covered my semi-nude body with the bed coverings. Shortly afterward, I heard his stomping approach.

"I know goddamn well you been drinkin' since I left!"

Had he already detected floating Vodka molecules in the living room? Jeez. I had drank half a fifth behind my closed door. I gave the dumbest reply: "I don't know what you're talking about."

Johnny Rahwaye's natural special effects face grew more distorted. "Get ya white ass up. Dress. Let's talk in the living room. Ain't gone be another time like this."

I nodded like a bobble headed toy, not certain what specific topic he had in mind for discussion. But I sensed I was in deep bat shit for breaking one of his house rules, let alone a more serious infraction deserving crueler punishment.

Now we resembled mortal enemies facing each other from the ends of a swayback couch.

"Zae, let's get this matter straight. You got a bottle hidden somewhere?"

"I did; honest. I finished it before you returned." Johnny was born with unbecoming Husky dog-pale eyes and they weren't buying my lie. "All was left was a shot glass worth."

"Yeah; right. Let me tell you something, bitch. I smell Vodka… smell it seepin' from your pores. I'm gonna fuck you up and kick your ass out for good."

"It won't happen again. I *promise!*" My contriteness sounded phony.

"Bullshit." He sprang to his full, imposing height of six feet. Face turning redder, fists on alert to attack. "Fuck you, 'ho!"

"Go jump in the Willamette River!" I trembled as I watched him march down the hallway to his bedroom. Was this the end of me? I thought. Brains splattered.

Having borrowed coins to buy Vodka was a moral issue I should have allowed myself to feel guilty about. Well, I wasn't. Why? Because I considered it justified revenge for all the times he verbally abused me, more so when *he* was drunk or sky high on a dangerous street drug. Forced sex was always his kinky desire when he wasn't sober. Seemed as though I was his sex slave on demand.

I secretly sipped more Vodka before I turned on the VCR and slid in a classic porn movie titled *Behind the Green Door*. Under Vodka's superb spell, I was feeling horny for sex but not with disgusting Johnny. I was leaning more toward pleasuring myself. As I was about to insert fingers, the bedroom door exploded open from his weight and gorilla anger.

"What's wrong with you?!" I rose on elbows. I challenged with a stare.

"Did you take coins outta here?" He was holding the underside of the tainted shoebox.

"Well, I…" Did I dare tell him the truth?

"Bitch, don't lie to me!"

"Well, I… a small loan is all."

"Fuck that, you worthless little piece of shit!"

"I'll pay it back. Just $20 bucks!"

"I oughta blow your head off!"

Johnny wrestled with the shoebox to gain proper leverage, and then he pitched hundreds of coins at my face. I scrambled to duck the shower of coin bullets; many smacked my face. I was too stunned to protest. Before I could say anything, he leaped onto the bed. Like a cowboy ready to alight on a saddle, he straddled my waist and pinned my arms to my sides.

"Didn't I warn you I was gonna fuck you up?"

Funny how fear stimulated my consciousness to a weird level, triggered strong vibrations in my ears, while all kinds of death images ping ponged in my brain. And when I witnessed him aim the long barrel of a Smith & Wesson .38, I was constricted for a brief moment from swallowing saliva. I knew I was doomed to become another Portland homicide statistic.

"Kill your sorry ass right now. Make it look like suicide!"

"I'm sorry, Johnny. I *swear*, I'll pay you back $20 before the weekend!" What he ordered me to do was a sure sign of impending homicidal rage.

"Open your fucking mouth!"

At the speed of light images of my parents, grandparents, and siblings flashed across my mind. Most knew my track record of abusive behavior associated with alcoholism. I hoped they wouldn't think I had finally succeeded at a bloody demise.

"Please don't hate me!" Tears rolled across my cheeks.

"Keep it open!"

With ruthless intent the tip of the gun barrel parted my trembling lips, forcing me to further open my mouth. The taste of old metal and preservation oil made my flesh crawl. My nerves were like disruptive bees on their beehive.

This known fool with an ugly misshaped face was going to shoot my lights out forever: a thirty-something alcoholic/drug addict loser. Incredibly – even under threat of imminent death – I still was willing to sacrifice more facets of my mental and physical health for alcohol. Without it, I couldn't properly challenge the hurdles and curve balls of pain from hereditary sources and from a hit and run crime.

I started mentally tripping about whether or not his Smith and Wesson .38 had already killed somebody, maybe another woman boozer whose investigation was in the hands of a Cold Case Investigation Squad.

Johnny cocked the trigger. "Tighten your lips around the barrel… yeah, suck on it!"

I gagged several times. Nothing about my reaction was a personal turn-on. I saw myself only as a hostage victim in fear of losing her life.

He continued clowning with me until he exhausted his supply of commands. I thought that was the end of the attack. He threatened to screw me – hard and fast, as if I were a despicable prostitute punching bag. That's exactly how he performed for what seemed like an hour's worth.

After he finished the rape, he punched me in the jaw so hard I somehow catapulted off the bed. Urine leaked from me as my face swelled, as he shouted an ultimatum: I had only one hour to pack up all of my property and vacate his apartment.

Oh well. I thought I was the real showdown winner because I wasn't going to repay him the loan. In spite of an achy swollen face and sore vagina, I was able to finish the remaining Vodka in peace! Calmed my jitters. Boosted my self-confidence. There was hope, after all.

"Sick bastard," I mumbled, but smiling like a happy drunk. I started crawling toward the bathroom. I needed to assess my injury, more than eager to greet tomorrow morning. An early hustle for cash to buy me another fifth or two of my favorite drink.

More personal wreckage was looming on multiple horizons and they seemed fated to happen to me. Was I the first human granted NINE LIVES? Imagine the complex complications of that possibility.

CHAPTER ONE

EARLY CHILDHOOD DYNAMICS

Conversations about a family's past can be triggered by various situations, from family reunions, funerals, weddings, road trips, to birthday parties, high school and college graduations. When I was old enough to understand family dynamics, I questioned my mother Louisa during the fourth day of Spring Break 1972. I was ten years old then. We loved gardening together, especially planting wild flower seeds in the ample backyard of our three-story house in Corvallis, Oregon. Such seeds would grow into summertime flowers indigenous to our Pacific Northwest Region. Their tantalizing fragrances would attract bees, butterflies, birds, and their spectrum of colors would make excellent table and window decorations.

I stopped and watched how she lovingly planted the seeds. "Mom, when I become an adult, how long should I wait until I have my own kids?" I had wanted to ask her that question since I turned seven. I was already aware of how babies were made. I wasn't so innocent and sheltered in that department.

Mom didn't skip a beat in her enjoyment; she didn't even look me in the eye when she replied, in her customary gentle toned voice, "Expect a major responsibility, child. Disallow yourself, in your adulthood, from getting pregnant too soon. You might regret it later in life."

I don't know why she chuckled after the warning. Did that mean she was holding back information about her pregnancy with me? I couldn't resist asking about how I was in her womb for nine months. What she revealed was new information I hadn't heard discussed before.

Without overemphasizing the past, she said she suffered enormous pain from birthing me because the dosage of anesthesia was inadequate. What made the birthing crisis more difficult was my earlier development: my feet were facing toward the uterus. That situation was a threat to my survival, thus an emergency C-section procedure was performed. My mom was in less danger, also.

The horrible image instilled some fear in my young mind. I didn't want to experience her traumatic child birthing. "How long were you in labor, Mom?"

"More hours than you have fingers."

"Wow. I was a bad baby to you. I'm sorry."

She chuckled, focused her green eyes into my similar green eyes, and stroked my right cheek with a dirt-smudged finger. I didn't erase the mark.

"Not your fault, honey. Difficult situations happen all the time... out of our control."

Days later, my mother offered another confession. We were lounging in the backyard patio festooned with a variety of hanging plants. My father Will the master mathematician was busy in the basement tinkering with a new complex equation that I would never be able to solve in a million years! He was the smartest member of our family. Before I started munching on my Hershey chocolate bar, I offered her half of it. She declined, with her characteristic teasing chuckle. My curiosity lit up like sparkles from fireworks.

Regularly eating too many sweet treats was her weakness during her pregnancy and that compulsion could have been a contributing factor to how I developed childhood food allergies. My severe asthma, for instance, started when I was two, exacerbated not only by food allergies, but by air-born allergies from house dust, mold, tree, grass and weed pollens. Also, I suffered from eczema, which goes along with asthma.

(In Chinese medicine, the lungs and skin are combined as one organ and problems with both are considered a sign of loss and grief.)

My frequent hospitalizations due to scary asthma attacks developed into episodes of pneumonia, also. During one particular stormy nighttime episode, my father cradled me in his arms, exited his truck, and rushed me to the emergency room entrance.

I was five years old. A light blue baby blanket covered my head, protecting me from breathing in cold air, which would exacerbate my asthma.

Bear with me, please, for a moment. My pediatrician had me on the following prescribed medications. Quadrinal, a brand name, consisted of the medications Ephedrine, Hydrochloride, Phenobarbital, Potassium Iodide and Theophylline Calcium Salicylate. The Quadrinal – for thinning lung mucous – was a thick, red, sticky liquid. I hated it because it tasted worse than Caster oil brewed from the Dark Ages. Even my bronchodilator contained ephedrine. Hydrocortisone cream helped reduce my eczema outbreaks and it's characteristic drive-you-mad-pull-out-your-hair itchiness.

I consumed Quadrinal four times a day for fifteen years. As a treatment for asthma, it also helped calm me but its phenobarbital component gave me the vividest dreams of my life. Furthermore, Quadrinal failed to control my most severe asthma attacks. Withdrawal from the drug, by the time I turned seventeen, caused me significant anxiety, depression, and perpetuated feelings of hopelessness. Can you imagine how my young brain would be damaged by that decade-plus consumption of a barbiturate? Can you imagine how long-term use of hydrocortisone would affect my body in various ways? Well, thinning of my skin was one.

My dedicated mom spent much time with me as an infant and toddler because of my *intrinsic* asthma (inherited) and *extrinsic* asthma (caused by climate changes and exacerbating emotional stress). Her time focused on my needs may have made my siblings feel unloved and abandoned… perhaps jealous. You'd think they would have shown me sympathy, at age four or five, whenever I held my breath in the presence of our mom so she wouldn't suspect I was having another asthma attack. Suppression sure didn't improve matters.

Sometimes I experienced two-hour long episodes of breathing hard before I would climb out of bed, alert my sleeping parents so they could transport me to the hospital. Because of life-threatening bouts with asthma, my maternal grandparents, Elizabeth and Samuel McKenzie, wanted me to live with them on their farm in Vale, Oregon. Their common sense reasoning: a less stressful environment might improve my health.

My parents often engaged in assaultive behavior against each other. I remember walking around, as if trying to avoid crushing eggshells, with the weight of anxiety and fear in me. In particular, my mom refused to relinquish her custody over me for the sake of good; my dad wanted a final solution rather than physical confrontations.

Later in my development, my pediatrician advised my contentious parents that I would never be physically active like other spunky kids my age. Her assessment only made me want to prove her wrong. I vowed to get *very* active, in spite of my asthma.

In retrospect, I give my parents credit for being bold and brave. At age five, they enrolled me in swimming lessons (at age four, I had previously learned to float). Mom also enrolled me in ballet class when I was six. As a child herself, she had wanted to take dance lessons but never got the opportunity.

The grade school years. Asthma continued to escalate my hospitalizations. My mom would write notes to my teachers explaining that because of inclement weather I needed to stay in the classroom during recess. Otherwise, my asthma would exacerbate. I benefited, though. I spent those recesses reading and writing stories and poetry. Alone, for many hours. That's how I developed reading and writing skills.

In spite of less time with classmates, I was voted as the third-grade female recipient of the Citizenship Award because I got along so well with others. The male recipient was Fred Glintzer.

I switched grade schools at the age of nine (fourth grade). The other kids targeted me for ridicule because of my awkward lack of eye to hand contact in games like foursquare. I just lacked the necessary experience needed for skillful ball control. I was also picked last for teams in physical education.

One time I had an asthma attack after running around the gym with my classmates. My sixth grade teacher was Mr. Charlie Munskin. I wondered why he had a habit of wrapping the end of his pant leg around his bony hairy leg while sitting on a stool in front of the class. After I had stopped running, he asked me, "Do you need to wipe your chops?" What did my "chops" have to do with me running out of breath?

All of the members in my immediate family had some allergic reactions such as eczema or other reactions such as asthma. My mom was allergic to her *own* bacteria and pet dander; imagine an overactive immune response to your own bacteria and pet dander causing sinusitis. My dad and sister had food allergies, which caused eczema, and they both had asthma in their later years. My sister Tess had asthma after the birth of her twins when she was 32. My dad also developed asthma when he was around 50. My brother had rashes like eczema but never was diagnosed with allergies.

At age 10, I developed my imagination particularly when I wrote a children's book entitled *Kewpie, Jot and the Happy Clown...* about a doll, a pink teddy bear and a clown. The three characters were all being pursued by a tiny warlock who lived in a mushroom. Mom typed it for me (grammatical errors and all) and I illustrated it, but never tried to publish it. From the age of six, I learned how to write poetry. One poem was entitled *Gray McBonkey, the Important Looking Donkey* which was one of my best childhood poems. Somehow, it got lost amongst storage boxes in the basement of my mom's house.

Everybody on our planet has been shaped by childhood experiences and how they shape our adulthood. I also played with wooden blocks and used them to create schools for all the stuffed animals my brother and I owned. We didn't focus much on the materials of those stuffed animals, upon which dust particles and other allergen agents would collect – having the potential to trigger another bout of asthma. Because we had so many of the stuffed ones, my parents decided that rubber-based toy animals would be better for my health.

"Head, Heart, Hands, and Health", that's the motto of 4-H, a network of youth organizations whose mission is engaging youth to reach their full potential while advancing the field of youth development. My participation in 4-H covered cooking and sewing; I learned similar skills in Camp Fire Girls. From ages 8 to 11, I took piano lessons. I shelved thousands of school library books. Participated in Girl Scouts, church youth group, and high school activities. Also, Rainbow for Girls (related to the Masons' organization) which involved performing community service.

When I was eighteen, I was deemed Worthy Advisor (leader of the Rainbow meetings) who organized bake sales and car washes to raise money for the Waverly Home for abused kids. In both middle school and high school, I went to Methodist church camp, Loon Lake, and became a one-week-in-the-summer camp counselor, at age 17, for younger kids.

What with this kind of wholesome character building foundation, you'd think it would become a solid firewall defense against any kind of future foolishness I would perpetrate against myself and other people, including family members and friends. Goes to show how The Dice of Fate can hand you unpredictable outcomes.

CHAPTER TWO

SUMMERTIMES ON THE DOUBLE HORSESHOE RANCH

Welcome to Vail, Oregon…population, as of 2023:1910.

This sleepy but progressive little city was for me an out-of-school-for-summer vacation paradise during my preteen/teen years (6-16). Fond memories, for sure. On a map, it is in the craggy shape of an upright rectangle and covers a stingy 1.4 square miles. It's in the county seat of Malheur, about 12 miles west of the Idaho border, and beyond to the intersection of U.S. Routes 20 and 26. A vehicular trip from Portland to Vale will take approximately 5 hours 56 minutes, if you go via Interstate 84East.

Plenty scenic beauty, charm, and history along the way. This territory marks the how and why of the Oregon Trail, where nonnative pioneers paved the way to further explore/exploit land-grabbing opportunities. Before such visions had manifested through their efforts, Native American tribes, like the Lamanite and Paiutes, were stewards of this territory for hundreds of years. Today, those tribes make up only a smaller percentage of Vale's population.

My grandparents, loving and supportive almost to a fault, were Elizabeth and Samuel McKenzie. Salt of the earth personalities who had fully embraced the farming mindset way back in the 1940s. Although their farm was much smaller than neighboring farms, I thought as a child that the twelve acres was plenty enough playground for me and my special friends – including chickens, pigs, cows, and dogs. At times, the devil got into me. I chased flocks of chickens and they scrambled like Keystone Cops every which a way to find safety from a wild child. However, Buddy Boy, a black Jersey Giant rooster, managed to peck at my right foot, causing enough pain to make me cry out *OUCH!* Other breeds served us well… the Orpingtons, the Cornishes, the Australorps.

My favorite among the pigs was Teddy. He was sweet, affectionate, smiley-faced, comical. I still think he thought he was more dog than pig. I taught him a few tricks. My favorite of the three was whenever I whistled for him to come to me, he'd make the weirdest snorting sounds as his tail wagged, as if powered by electricity, and he'd roll over onto his back, then wait for me to massage his underside. I can hear his squeals of delight; goosebumps are creeping up my arms right now.

Vacationing on my grandparents' farm for two weeks each summer taught me about life and living. What an education! About having compassion for animals that help keep humans alive and well. My temporary residency wasn't all fun and games. Made me feel like a tomboy, especially whenever I was allowed to drive the smallest of the four plowing tractors. I still suffered from asthma and the medications I took helped a lot, but that didn't keep me from carrying out farm chores. I milked obedient cows and hoisted bucketfuls. I fed the grateful chickens and collected their gift of eggs. I pitched hay, as if I were born to perform that kind of labor. Fruit trees, mostly red apples and pears, awaited my harvesting assistance. Sometimes, I climbed ladders. Sometimes, I used a special telescopic picking pole.

Grandpa raised beef cattle and sugar beets. He had a heifer that was a pet and me and my practical joker cousin Carla would walk on its back. We collected the chicken eggs, named the hatched fluffy yellow chicks according to a unique characteristic of each one. Not a benign affair, though, when we scalded dead chickens (ooh my… Stinksville) and plucked their feathers.

Carla and I would set siphons (water distribution contraptions) in the ditches for the sugar beets. Grandpa had a garden from which we harvested vegetables. We would have "restaurants" where Carla and I would make a menu and then grandma would order her menu selections. Ants on logs was a favorite: raisins stacked on celery sticks with peanut butter speared along their middles.

We played "restaurant" with grandpa where we made menus for lunch and prepared them. One afternoon, he came to the house for lunch. He scolded us when he said, "Where's the darn meat, girls? A man needs MEAT!"

"You can eat meat tomorrow, grandpa," I replied, cocking my head.

Carla's reply was stoked with sassiness. "Yah, gramps. A one-day strike won't hurt you. I don't eat meat *everyday*. Geez."

We got much pleasure from playing with my mom's clay dolls. We put finely crafted dresses on them which my great grandma Bonnie had sewn using articulate tiny stitches. We played with my mom's petite glass and ceramic animals and made a village with them on the basement pool table.

My grandpa's love, respect, and affinity for animals was a prominent hereditary trait which I also found in myself at an early age. But an unfortunate mistake took the life of his beloved Irish Setter Rusty, at age eight. Grandpa and friends were on a hunting adventure for deer (other times they would hunt moose, pheasant, antelope, chucaars, quail). Somehow, Rusty got lodged in underbrush, camouflaging his body. Grandpa assumed the sudden movement was a deer, so he aimed and fired a single rifle shot. It killed Rusty instantly; a devastating injury to his head. That day marked the first time I had seen grandpa cry in my presence. He was a proud, strong-willed, self-respecting man. His grief for months was profound. Eventually he healed but the tragedy still left a figurative hole in his heart.

I had grieved with him, too, because I loved Rusty so much. My future self would experience the untimely deaths of pet companions I loved and cherished. We would "rescue" each other from challenging times... at my worst downfalls.

At night, when summer weekend skies were clear and stars hovered in the millions it seemed to me, Vale was more magical because of the overall sense of peace and tranquility stretched over the land in any direction. Elsewhere, humans were dying from wars, car crashes, inner-city street violence; women were fighting for equal rights, abortion rights, civil rights, and breaking through the glass ceilings of biased corporations. I, too, would be marked with an X. My cousin Carla Donahue, one year older than me, was born to be a prankster. Her sense of humor was off the charts. She was Twiggy-the-model skinny in a lithe frame. She had a slight limp in her right leg caused by a roll over car crash on Interstate 84; her dad, a construction foreman, was the driver but he didn't survive. Her eyes, a vivid blue, were almost shaped in a natural squint – as if she lost her bifocal eyeglasses and had to read print up close. A mop of unremarkable dark brown hair just barely draped to her earlobes. She got teased too much because her upper teeth protruded beyond the norm. But what fascinated me more was her fast track physical maturing. My budding breasts, along with Carla's, still wouldn't match the circumference and pointedness of Pam's breasts. We, Carla and I, wondered what kind of sex scandal would show itself on the horizon, by the time she would turn eighteen.

Just before dusk in late July of 1973, I suggested to visiting friend Pam that we play a game of Cops and Robbers with prankster Carla who was eleven years old. Unlike what Pam and I had in mind, Carla was none the wiser that Saturday. Our ample friend had to be an imaginary cowgirl arrested for robbing the town's only bank, because she failed to win at the start up game of Pitch Your Coin Closest To The Line (vertical) already made on a flat surface or an artificial one. She failed at three attempts.

Now our "criminal" stood stock-still, overly obedient but apprehensive.

"No way out of this, you dirty robber," I warned Carla, watching me loop more aged and fraying rodeo rope around her upper body, while Pam was honey bee busy working her weaker clothesline around Carla's ankles and thighs.

"That's enough, you guys," Carla said, in a whinny tone. "I didn't agree to look like a rope mummy."

Pam and I giggled.

"Don't *worry;* you're in good hands." I shot a mischievous glance at my partner. We exchanged winks. "Isn't that right, Deputy Pam?"

Pam tried to imitate actor John Wayne's iconic voice. "Sure is, Deputy Zae."

"*Wait!* Come on… Where you taking me?" A swell of panic protruded Carla's eyes but not much.

A large sack of potatoes was easier to carry.

After clumsy maneuvering, we managed to lift her. The next struggle happened when we started walking her to an air-filled rubber mattress I used for sunbathing. It was situated near a fancy, white brick-lined garden plot of mixed perennial flowers and manicured grass.

"I'm ready to quit this!" Carla whipped her head back and forth, resisting duct tape from covering her mouth. "Stop this game right now!"

"We'll make sure you can still breathe!" Like heartless dungeon torturers we laughed at her predicament. I wanted to punish her for her past pranks that had caused me great embarrassment and, to some extent, reducing my self-confidence as a girl who wanted to grow up to be a successful adult, mother, wife, and professional in whatever field I would endeavor.

Meanwhile, my farm-devoted grandparents were too busy with work to take any notice of our pleasurable fun. We promised Carla we would return within fifteen minutes.

"You better!"

I took another glance back at her. She looked like a giant caterpillar jerking and twisting and bucking to break free.

"I'll hate you forever, if you don't! You too, Pam!"

Between laughing our heads off and waving good-bye to our pretend prisoner, we already had decided to return much later. What we didn't expect was her terror-filled screams for help when we didn't return until almost an hour later. Her reddened, twisted face was wet with tears. Her hair was matted and damp. She had screamed so much that her lips had chapped and turned a faint purple.

By now, Grandma Liz's concern was in full throttle. Her complexion was ruddy. She was gray-haired, with a ramrod straight body firm from accustomed hard labor and who was an excellent baker of pies and cookies. She stomped a dusty work boot and demanded we release our poor friend from her merciless predicament. Her voice reflected

Christian values as she chided us for taking fun to the extreme, and warned us never do it again.

No joke. Carla's trauma was *real*. She was a fountain of tears, even after her mother returned to pick her up. A second consideration made me realize that we could have given her a heart attack or triggered suffocation. She was ticked off enough not to want to play with us for a very long time. Her rejection of us as playmates hurt me more than it did Pam. I suppose what I learned from that experience was this: never take true friendship for granted. If you do, it could bite you in the butt and leave you wondering what happened.

Years later, I would have a similar experience meant to end my life. Slam. Bam. No Thank You, Ma'am. The perpetrator might have rationalized what he did: what at first seemed like some kind of twisted, erotic joke, but my panic and feeling of doom would feel much like Carla's.

My empathy gene trait for animals expressed itself again when I was five years old. Me and my siblings cared for guinea pigs. One was Heidi, belonging to my older sister Tess. I wasn't Heidi's primary caretaker. Only once did my sister place Heidi under my care for a while when Tess had an extended visit at our grandparents' farm. What happened to Heidi was a damn shame and illustrated to me how easily people can ignore common sense and not focus on consequences of their behavior – whether intentional or unintentional.

That late-October day in Corvallis was blistery and colder than average compared to past Octobers. Matthew, the son of one of my mom's friends, was a visitor to our home. He was a cute, freckle face kid with curly red hair. He was antsy, entering and exiting through the kitchen door multiple times... as if the outdoors was beckoning him for a magical adventure. Heidi loved our roomy kitchen space because of the wonderful smells from food, baked goods, stored seasonings, indoor plants, and my mom's humming. All good, but Matthew's restlessness created a colder draft effect.

Later in the evening, I noticed Heidi wasn't displaying her usual spunky personality. Her refusal to eat her favorite food scraps in a bowl concerned me.

Two days later, her mysterious predicament hadn't improved, so my mom and I felt compelled to take her to a senior vet familiar to our family. His diagnose: poor Heidi had developed *pneumonia* that quickly! From just a drafty kitchen!

I was determined to spend all of my free time nursing Heidi back to excellent health. Like an ambitious TV chef, I blended the best curative vegetables available with her medicine. I used a special syringe to spurt the mixture into her mouth. With a cocky-like smile, I felt confident she would improve overnight.

Didn't happen.

A few days later, my mom insisted dad and I accompany her to a theater play reading of *When Justice Throws The Second Stone*. Before we departed, he urged that it would be best to turn off the heat lamp above Heidi's makeshift recuperation crate; he foresaw the possibility of a fire starting. A mistake.

Heidi was too fragile from the delay in her treatment and lack of steady heat. By the time we returned, she had died. Our immediate family was emotionally crushed and depressed; my sister in particular. Heidi's premature death triggered the first known asthma attack in Tess — that's how strong her grief had escalated.

We couldn't divorce ourselves from nurturing another guinea pig. We loved them. We named him Binny. He was cool in attitude until he started chewing on his wooden crate, whittling it down in sections which afforded him the opportunity to romp freely. Even graze in the living room.

We had no other choice but to secure him in a bigger crate, lessening the possibility of him chewing it to pieces. What happened next was a cruelty of fate. A little confusing too. Because he didn't chew on the upper regions of the new crate, his teeth grew longer and he couldn't properly drink water. He died from dehydration!

I was stomping foot pissed at that age but much motivated to start researching about the proper care and sustainability of guinea pigs. We named the next one *Zachary*. He was somewhat spastic; he would leap in the air and twitch. Weird behavior. I still have no explanation for it.

Through no fault of his own, Zachary was the cause of my having worsening allergies: itchy, teary eyes all day, every day. And causing me to suffer more asthma bouts. Was difficult to return him to his disappointed breeder. Another loss of a four-legged loved one.

CHAPTER THREE

DANCES WITH MEDICATION COCKTAILS

By the time I turned eighteen, I was convinced that my allergen and asthma conditions would plague my life until my demise, be the cause of it. As if I were locked in a prison cell on the moon and the warden himself had welded rebar steel over the hinges. No peace. No escape. Like I mentioned earlier, my entire family suffered similar bouts of allergen contamination but why was I so prone to be the most targeted family member? None of them consumed the percentage of medication cocktails prescribed for me. Sooner or later, cocktail remedies would become too powerful and destructive.

Suffering from pain on an almost daily basis inspired me to conduct my own research for a cure. Already, my allergists had warned me that no such cure existed but that experimentation with trial drugs was an ongoing process.

My handicap, so to speak, didn't stop my love of long distance running and swimming while I attended Corvallis High School. Twice weekly, preferably during spring and summer months, I ran alone five mile distances... on sidewalks and on asphalted streets – 35th Street was a favorite route. I was emboldened to swim the equivalent of two miles... at least three times a week during summer months.

Somehow, those activities expanded my lung capacity, reduced my stress levels, gave me hope for the future, and boasted my morale. I even imagined myself as a scientist scholar crusader traveling all over the world in search of ancient-old herbs that would yield cures for asthma.

I did, however, visit various Oregon public libraries (including the Multnomah County flagship in downtown Portland) and logged onto the Internet. The year was 1975. I discovered more information about the complexity of chemicals I had been taking for eighteen years, at that point in my life. There were extensive investigative studies and trials about oral corticosteroid use in severe asthma episodes. The costly and burdensome side effects? Frightening, like in let's create a new-age Frankenstein for symptoms relief. Long-term use of cortcosteriod could produce *weight gain, diabetes, osteoporosis, glaucoma, anxiety, depression, cardiovascular disease, immunosuppression, and adrenal insufficiency.* Lord have mercy! That menu was *worst* than having asthma itself. Goodbye, corticosteroid! I did gain weight and suffered mild osteoporosis later.

Surely, a potential future pregnancy would have negative effects on my fetus leading up to birthing. Heavy odds stacked against her or him, already. Remember what I revealed about my mother eating tons of sweets during her pregnancy, and the end results? All those tongue-twisting, consult-your-dictionary ingredient names on the back of candy packages. (Corn syrup is a universal ingredient in most candies, along with dyes.) The consensus amongst allergists was that the use of oral corticosteroid should be minimized.

Furthermore, I discovered that every asthma sufferer do not take the same medicine. Some sufferers take medicines that can be inhaled, or breathed. Some sufferers can take a pill. Asthma medicines are available in two types: quick relief to control the symptoms of an asthma attack and long-term control.

I had experienced more asthma attacks than anybody else in my family. In 2020, a statistical chart showed that over 3,000,000 Californians were asthma sufferers. I guess we Oregonians, in comparison, are lucky. More rain here than there; less pollutants and allergens to harm you.

Before I reveal that scariest episode, I want to express to you the love and respect I had for Masha and Dasha, lamb twins procreated on my grandpa's Double Horseshoe farm. I was twelve years old. On that sunny Saturday morning around eight I watched their mother Tammy bring them into the world. What a fantastic experience! They were our first twins and looked typical of the domesticated Valais Blacknose breed (having course off-white wool and round black patches spread over their knees) which first originated from the Valais region of Switzerland. 4-H members, those adult leaders and youth followers, would have been proud of them.

I was no naive part time farm girl about the slaughter of animals for food and for collateral goods – culminating in much needed profits. All those years I had "vacationed" there I disallowed myself to be a witness to the slaughter of our four-legged creatures. I had too much attachment to them, even the chickens.

When Masha and Dasha turned six months old, I had my first emotional blowout with Grandpa Will who, in his justified stubbornness, had already set a schedule for the slaughter of those particular animal friends. They weren't just farm animals, they were family members. I was willing to sacrifice anything to rescue them.

In the cinder block tool shed adjacent to the well-kept slaughter building, I watched grandpa sharpening trusted boning knives, with a determined gleam in his green eyes; another family trait. He taught me about two boning methods for lamb: tunnel and butterfly. Either method saved and showcased the integrity of said meat. Anything less than that goal would get you bad-mouthed criticism.

"Grandpa, please." I stood near him, my arms folded in defiance.

"Quit ya buggin' me, gal."

I watched how his jaw muscles twitched in a gesture of frustration and slow-burn anger. "Let me take care of them. You got others to slaughter."

Air gushed through his prominent nostrils. A few hairs protruded.

"If I got attached to every darn creature on this farm – except Rusty, we'd lack the necessary protein to sustain our own lives. Always understand, okay, that those two are meant to be meat producers – *only* that."

"I know, but..." Further words got stuck in my throat and I could feel my eyes misting, building up to tears. I could cry a bucket worth of them and still grandpa would neither be impressed nor deterred. He was unmovable.

Scrap-scrap-scrap went his expert sharpening on a whetstone.

"Let me buy them, grandpa!" The silence that followed seemed eerie, like a silent, mysterious gunslinger coming to a town to do battle with the sheriff. Had I struck a raw root canal nerve in Grandpa Will?

He turned, focused on my surly face, and shook his head. Was he pitying me?

"Zae, come to your senses. I ain't a farmer for nothin'. I own every creature on the Double Horseshoe. And don't you forget that. Stamp it on your forehead."

His response seemed so cold and cruel, completely the opposite of what I was feeling. Did I dare argue in further defense of Masha and Dasha?

I jumped up and down several times before I shouted, "A thousand dollars, grandpa! That should be enough." In reality, as a preteen, I had only $62 in my savings account.

"*Go, child!*" His finger loomed like an arrowhead. "Get ya lil' butt outta here. I'll deal with you later!"

The weight of his reprimand slumped my shoulders in defeat as I considered Masha's and Dasha's fate after their inevitable slaughter.

Dinnertime a week later. Already, I had disdain for our processed beef liver, mostly because of how my mom cooked slices to an unappetizing leathery blackness: overcooked. I wasn't exactly forced to eat it, but my grandparents shamed me by mentioning the countless sacrifices they had made and how poor parents in poor countries (particular emphasis on Africa, China, and India) had starving kids who would kill for mom's style of cooking beef liver.

Now I was another kind of victim, staring at the broiled body parts of Masha and Dasha! Laid out on a jumbo platter to serve five of us at the dinner table. I wanted to puke. I wanted to slap grandpa's weather-beaten face. I wanted to stomp my feet until they reamed holes in the floor. No one at the dining table was going to force me to eat what remained of my friends.

Armed with enough courage and more disgust, I jerked to my feet, stormed away in tears, slammed the bedroom door, and almost did a swan dive onto my quilt-covered bed.

I must have cried for hours because my eyes were sore, red, and swollen when I awakened. Throughout the transition, no family member present that day came to my rescue to help elevate my deep pain from grief.

My scariest asthma attack happened when I was arrested for drunk driving. The year was 1997, and I was 35 years old. Skies were overcast all day long. I already had finished a fifth of vodka but craved for another fifth. I was more than tipsy but not blindingly drunk, so I thought. The less-than-reliable car I was driving needed break repair on each hub. That predicament was scary enough, especially when you needed to take a sudden push on the brake pedal and what you'd get in return was surface to surface contact – in other words, no brake pedal resistance. Sometimes, though, if you pumped like crazy you could *force* a stop and not clobber the rear of another vehicle ahead of you.

Oh no. Didn't stop my pursuit to the nearest liquor store. I got what I craved and I was heading back home to my husband Tim. (He was addicted to alcohol, too, and as you will later discover, his assaultive behavior would flourish.) Why he didn't raise hell in the first place and take the car's keys from me still remains a mystery.

Home was only five blocks away. Vodka stimulation was catching up with me; I was "floating" in the driver's seat, feeling no pain, and eager to finish the second fifth.

I was doing great until I saw the white car ahead of me, about to break for the traffic signal turning Red. I squinted, misjudging a safer stopping distance. Like an active piston in an engine block, I started pumping the break peddle until it kissed the floorboard. I gripped the steering wheel in a chokehold. Every muscle in my body was prepared for the inevitable crash. I believe I was traveling at least 40 miles per hour. Honking the horn as a warning didn't help, either. In my drunken state, I could determine the driver was hunched low, like some short statued senior citizen drivers who can barely see over the steering wheel.

Before I could pump the horn again, my front end slammed against the white car's rear. The sounds of metal against metal was bone chilling and very scary. I saw how the driver's gray-haired head was whiplashed back and forth. I thought I heard her scream. That's what made me panic, scared me to death, and then I decided to haul tail out of the intersection as other cars refused to travel.

I couldn't allow the police to intervene and order me to take a sobriety test. Right? Failure was guaranteed. I decided to pilot around her victimized car, took a left turn, and sped away to a familiar back street where the utility lighting was poorer. Dense with pine trees.

In my haste to escape liability, I took too sharp a turn into the next street. I plowed toward the sidewalk, bounced off a parked SUV, and catapulted a curbside mailbox. My head banged against the steering. Blood spurted from my nostrils. The impact was so violent it stalled the engine and deflated the front right tire.

Only two blocks away from home!

Ear-splitting sirens growing louder, closer!

I was screwed, as neighbors – gawking in disbelief and fearing the worst, began pouring out of their residences.

Less than a minute later, four police cruisers performed a "we've pinned you in with a tactical maneuver, asshole", keeping me from escaping a second time. What would happen next should have instantly cured me from abusing alcohol, forever… but my addictions, oh boy, were mighty powerful negative engines.

CHAPTER FOUR

A HARD HEAD MAKES A SORE BUTT

Yes in deed… in the Clackamas County Jail, where I was booked an hour later for DUI, Hit and Run, and Reckless driving. By now, I didn't know which was about to make me puke: the reality of arrest and forthcoming consequences or the lingering effects of my drunkenness. I was a mess, with dried blood splattered here and there on my leather jacket and blouse; cotton balls stuffed into my nostrils to prevent more blood drainage; and a head of hair that resembled a Bartum & Bailey clown's fright wig. Never had I felt utterly finished as a human being. A big fat whopping failure – again.

The booking officers, beefy brutes, knew I was disabled by alcohol, so why was it still necessary to give me a damn sobriety test? Just book me, write it up as a give-me, and set a court date. No way could I plead innocent to all of the charges. Get it over with, was what I wanted so I could reunite with Tim. I felt certain he had gone bananas his own way when I failed to return home with the second fifth of vodka, most likely locked up safely somewhere as evidence to be used against me in court. Perhaps he would be happier to hear the bad news.

From the reception "tank" (where new detainees are lodged together, unless they are a serious threat to themselves or others) I was escorted to a small steel enclosure built to hold a single occupant. Faint body odors prevailed. Harsh overhead lighting revealed graffiti epitaphs and declarations of undying love. The steel door featured an opening with only three slats for air circulation; not good for viewing whatever was on the outside of the corridor. I could hear other female detainees crying and laughing and bitching with profanity about their plights.

As sinus pain pressure in my head escalated, as I became more sober, I stared at the god-awful bunk bed welded in place. On top of it was a pathetically skinny plastic covered mattress showcasing a multitude of wear cracks that could scratch your bare skin. In comparison, a yoga mat was more inviting and comforting.

I tried to convince myself that this claustrophobic sardine can was only a temporary nightmare, that I would be freed from it soon.

An hour later, I reflected on how I got myself in this predicament. I could have killed myself or the innocent senior citizen driver I smashed into. All because of my addiction to vodka. Without that fifth in my system the crimes wouldn't have occurred. Although this marked my first DUII, I was otherwise a responsible defensive driver. For sure, my insurance company would be pissed and if I stayed in jail too long, my job would be in jeopardy.

I forced myself to sit on the cool mattress. I stared at the steel door, hoping it would magically open in the next five minutes. I hugged myself because chills went through me. That sinus pressure was building and I had to breathe through my mouth; the inside of it was drying, making swallowing less saliva harder.

Every nerve in my body pulsed with tingly, burning sensations. I scrambled off the mattress and began pacing. I could tell my blood pressure was sky high, but I couldn't calm myself. The more I paced, the more my anxiety level soared.

At this point, I began wheezing because I couldn't ingest more oxygen. I tried harder to suck in more of it. Sounds from the other detainees seemed to explode in my head. Fearing the worst, I started pounding on the steel door. Repeatedly I shouted "I'M HAVING AN ASTHMA ATTACK. HELP ME. SOMEBODY!"

Hyperventilation was draining my energy as I pounded the steel door with my right foot and right hand. My eyes grew blurrier. Why was my mind playing tricks on me? I thought I was entombed in the belly of a thrashing killer whale. My throat felt like a psycho had stuffed a wool sock down to the hilt.

"WOMAN DOWN!!" came alarmed shouts from other detainees.

To save my life from another asthma attack, I pounded harder with both fists. That's when I heard jangling keys and multiple footsteps racing along the corridor.

"What's your problem, Rankin?" said a frowning female jailer, seemingly dismissing my obvious aggravated condition.

"I'm having... can't breathe... I got... asthma... getting worse." I lowered to my knees, gasping for any amount of air to enter my lungs. Craving the rescue of a bronchodialator. "I have... a history of..."

"Ahh. You're just having a typical panic attack. Relax. It'll end soon."

"You'll be okay, honey," said another jailer.

I hated her patronizing grin. "Not a panic attack; it's ASTHMA!" My wheezing was at a dangerous level. Blood was draining from my brain. My face. Weakness stabbed at my entire body. Clouds of darkness were approaching and I would be gobbled up in it. I was losing consciousness.

The faces of authority staring at me were more hideous looking – like in the Freddy Krueger character of the movie *A Nightmare on Elm Street* – than human. I despised their ignorance, their lack of compassion. The arrival of a nurse didn't improve matters. Either she was equally clueless or faked it.

Only when I started turning bluish in the face and jerking from epileptic-like spasms did one of the jailers radio for a gurney to rush me to the infirmary.

Literally I was *half-dead* on arrival.

The infirmary staff didn't transport me to the nearest hospital until they attached an oxygen oximeter (measures the amount of oxygen you should be receiving in your blood and flowing to other essential body parts) to my right middle finger. The results? Only 50% capacity! How my symptoms were broadcast in the steel sardine can grew twice as worst while an ambulance purposely crawled to a designated hospital.

A doctor there gave me a nebulizer treatment and two 20 milligrams of the steroid pill prednisone. Said dose was a third *lower* than the usual dose of prednisone that I would take whenever I experienced acute asthma. Two hours later, I was heaving again. A nurse, mentioning to me she also was an asthma sufferer, failed at setting up the nebulizer because she lacked knowledge of how that particular brand should work. Sounds crazy, I know, but true. My limited layman's knowledge worked like a blessing and I administered it to myself. I survived to greet the following stormy morning, my second day in jail.

Somehow, the Winds of Fate blew me in the right direction. My forthcoming court punishment would be lightweight: two-day jail sentence; a $1000 fine; a six-month diversionary program commitment; abstinence from any kind of alcoholic beverage until all court orders were fulfilled. I had wanted to show the lady judge and the victim how sorry and repentant I was when I asked the judge if I could perform community service work… maybe for ailing senior citizens (my victim was age 83, a retired clinical psychologist) managing to live independent lives, maybe for at-risk teen girls who needed a compassionate mother figure in their lives. The judge thought that kind of volunteerism was commendable but suggested I could seek-out such opportunities on my own time. I agreed. I pursued becoming a volunteer for voting registration.

Remember the adage "A HARD HEAD MAKES A SORE BUTT?"

My near-death experience still didn't teach me enough about the inherit dangers of alcohol addiction. A twisted, incomparable, more vicious competitor was on the horizon from South American cartels and its outrageous popularity would eventually kill/incarcerate millions of people worldwide.

The ultimate early-80s street drug. *CRACK COCAINE!* I, too, would became its victim… saw it as a temporary fix for my extrinsic asthma (derived from stress, anxiety, environmental issues). The biggest misconception of my life.

CHAPTER FIVE

HIGHER EDUCATION AND ADVENTURE ABROAD

It was the summer of my junior year in high school. The year was 1979. I was a role model for community service and a Rainbow for Girls Worthy Adviser (leader of the meetings). The organization was affiliated with the Fraternal Order of Masons. I was one of many youth volunteer fundraisers for good causes, like managing volunteer teams for car washes and bake sales. Money raised would help support the Waverly Home for Abused Kids. I was also a Grand Officer for Hawaii at the Rainbow for Girls Grand Assembly.

During that same summer, I worked on the Litter Patrol picking up litter along the highways between Corvallis and Albany. I liked the job because it was outdoors under the warming rays of the sun. The uniform for this job included a bright orange plastic mesh vest, a yellow hard hat, and hiking boots. During lunch breaks, I would often crave either peanut butter and cheddar cheese sandwiches or peanut butter and cottage cheese sandwiches.

Before I graduated from Corvallis High School in June 1980, I worked part-time at a new Wendy's location in Corvallis. I maintained the salad bar and sometimes worked behind the counter serving burgers and other menu items. The manager there disrespected me by pinching my butt, as if he was inspecting the ripeness of a pear, as if the sexist gesture was an obligation. But I was reluctant to report him to corporate headquarters.

After high school graduation (freedom from what my brother and I called "Hassle School" because of student bullies' behavior against us) I was busy working for the Forrest Service in a President Jimmy Carter supported program called Youth Conservation Corps. Employment in YCC was done by a lottery system – if they picked your name, you had a summer job. Mine was located on the beach at Reedsport, Oregon.

We did clear cutting with axes, stream stabilization, trail maintenance, and built a footbridge. I enjoyed this outdoor routine, although I had a severe asthma attack due to allergies. They caused my hospitalization. On one occasion, I was pruning bushes on the beach. Somehow, a twig scratched the surface of my right eye and scraped off its outer cells. Seemed like the pain was a level 15; I was subscribed pain pills. I had to wear an eye patch. I discontinued my assignment for almost a week.

In September 1980, I started my first college experience at Christian-based Seattle Pacific University. My minister had written me a recommendation for enrollment. What another challenging experience! I first thought of majoring in Philosophy and/or Linguistics. I enjoyed my Philosophy professor because he was flexible in his personality and wasn't a staunch, step-on-your-neck educator. He was my favorite professor because of his astute understanding and insightful way he taught lessons.

Among the students, he would call out my name and ask me about something related to today's lesson. He'd laugh because I would be in a drowsy nod, requiring him to awaken me. I didn't think he knew I was a devoted member of the university's rowing crew team. Practice was from 5 am to 7 am. After that kind of grueling workout, I wanted nothing more than a period of rest.

Being on the crew team was great exercise for me. There was a spiritual quality about it – out on Lake Washington rowing through the black, still water and keeping perfect rhythm with other rower's oars slicing methodically through water. The rhythm and quiet push and pull of the oars was peaceful and serene.

I had the strong quadriceps required of women rowers, focusing on the push from the legs rather than just the upper body to move smoothly and powerfully through the water. I had endurance more than speed in my rowing, having been a ballet dancer for 12 years. In crew, power with the oar behind the water as well as speed are what won the three-minute race – won by only inches between the sculls (boats) competing.

My second and third years in college were at Southern Oregon State College where I changed my major to English. I was also studying French at the time as I had in high school. Ashland, Oregon was beautiful with rolling hills and Emigrant Lake was a short bike ride from the campus and that is where I would go to swim in summertime. One time I swam for two hours and got a second-degree burn on my face from swimming on my back. When I got out of the water, I saw a bearded male stranger loading my bike onto the cargo bed of his truck.

"Hey! *Stop!* That's my bike; I need it to make it back home!" The apparent thief seemed not to have a care in the world. No shame, no guilt, just a cold stare before he decided to return my property to the pavement. I didn't want to project fear as I focused on the hunting knife attached to his belt. Was he one of those hate women psychos?

"Next time, sweetie, buy you a damn lock." He threw my bike onto the ground; it survived the assault. I wanted to hit him with a rowing oar, if I had one available.

I stomped a foot. "You got a truck, mister. You don't need my bike!" He flipped me the finger, climbed into the driver's seat, then after firing up the engine, he burned rubber. Shaking my head, I watched him speed away. I wasn't going to allow him to ruin the rest of my day.

When that incident happened during my first summer at SOSC, I was living with 60-year-old widow Mrs. Greta Popovich who lived in a quaint two-story house. The lake was six miles from Emigrant Lake. I lived in the upstairs bedroom, which was the whole floor, long enough to dance in. I had a single bed and it was partly enclosed from the rest of the room with a bookcase against the wall where I put both my anthologies of English and American Literature and books (one for my French class, the other for my Animal Behavior class among others). I also had a small black and white TV at the foot of the bed on a stand.

I had a record player I used to play the score of the movie *Papillion* (meaning butterfly in French). A table and chair were available to me, if I wasn't at the campus library.

All through college, at SPU, SOSC and later U of O, I worked in the libraries and in the college and university cafeterias as a server and cashier. For me, dorm living was okay my first year at SOSC. My short-term roommate Claresa had her left eye permanently shut because of a birth defect. She didn't share more information about her misfortune.

We weren't compatible. She put me in an awkward situation whenever she invited her boyfriend over to socialize (almost always). Even when she wasn't on her period she was temperamental and testy... most likely attributed to mutual lack of privacy. She had a habit of bitching about "her yeast infection prevented her from having sex with her boyfriend...." Don't think I wasn't grateful when she decided to leave and live with him. I hope her yeast infection days are over!

Before we journey across the seas leading to France – where I would study the French language and culture – I have another brief anecdote to share with you. As a SOSC freshman, I had an English professor who taught me about the craft of writing fiction and rules of punctuation. Richard (not his birth name) was a fiction writer whom I thought I was in love with. Don't ask me why; it was just one of those things. Perhaps a romantic dumb illusion. We didn't socialize outside of the classroom. He had promised to stay in touch via correspondence. And he kept that promise.

We reunited and ended up attending a Shakespearian Playhouse production in Ashland, Oregon. I remember how much Richard praised my skills needed for written English assignments. I had focused on e.e. Cummings' poems; Richard gave me an A+ for that assignment and said it was "brilliant". I usually earned A's in all of my English writing and literature classes.

One of my favorites was the assignment I wrote on a poem by Samuel Taylor Coleridge. My dad the mathematician, who in general doesn't offer compliments most of the time, stunned me when he praised my Coleridge paper: "Honey, this is *excellent*... better than your siblings' writing." Hearing that come from him was special and heartwarming. His rare compliment rang in my head for days.

After studying French for four years in high school and two years at SOSC, I got accepted into the overseas program where I went to Poitiers, France. I could barely restrain my eagerness for the challenges ahead, saying goodbye to my mom while the Mother hen in her fussed over my medical issues (asthma in particular) and feeling I wasn't fully prepared to deal with them in a foreign country. Didn't lessen her concerns over the fact that I had allergy serum and could give myself shots in France. In other ways, I was prepared: remembering to take my diaphragm because I was still a vulnerable virgin who didn't want an early-in-life pregnancy.

September 1983. My girlfriends Kendall and Dione joined in celebrating my 21st birthday. We weren't like hell-bound party animals, but kept our cools with low alcohol content rosé wine. Three bottles! We giggled a lot that day. They also were traveling overseas to become students at the same University. After instructors tested our knowledge of French at the OSSHE (Oregon State System of Higher Education) program orientation, the decision was made to enter us in to the second level of classes where we would study French with other foreign students in similar programs. The first level was elementary understanding of the language, compared to the third level that was for the most knowledgeable students who were directly enrolled with other French students. For example, Geraldine, my friend since First Grade, was a high achiever of spoken and written French. Subsequently, she migrated to Quebec, Canada, where she used her fluency in French and obtained a PhD in Art History.

The end of orientation! We went hitchhiking for three days, meeting various drivers who spoke French. A particular laundry truck driver picked us up on the third day when he saw us dancing on the side of the road. Perhaps the image of a fun-loving, freewheeling trio of American girls was going to turn into reality on the spot and make his unspoken sexual fantasies come to fruition. His attitude of wishful thinking dwindled like hot candle wax after our travel weary minds and bodies needed much recuperation. All along the travel route, we were nodding out like heroin addicts.

That third day we decided to travel by train from the border of France into Italy. On the train, Kendall met Dominique, a flirtatious Italian. I thought they had instant attraction chemistry. He invited us to meet his parents who lived in the historically famous city of Pisa, best known as the home of the architectural wonder The Leaning Tower of Pisa. We experienced up close the gravity-defying structure. His parents were very gracious and hospitable and let us stay for several days... would have been longer if it was his decision to make. Maybe that was because he admired her athletic killer legs, short blond hair, and big blue eyes.

His gregarious mother was determined to feed us delicious meals, like her style of spaghetti and sausage preparation. I suppose she was trying to fatten us because she said we looked "too skinny". Dione and I got "fat" while Kendall missed out on some of those five meals a day because she was more focused on Dominique than her appetite.

It came time to depart from such a lovely family. We didn't want to overstay our welcome. Besides, we had to return to France to pursue our education.

The classes we had varied from French Literature to History and were all spoken in French – no exceptions; making the learning process more challenging. I excelled in the French Literature classes, spoke up often when we studied Marguerite Yourcenar, Albert Camus, Simond de Beauvoir, and others.

One of my French Literature professors approached the Head of the OSSHE Program and expressed the opinion that I was "gifted" in understanding the literature. Hearing that made me feel really good. Although I knew my grammar wasn't perfect, she still understood all that I was trying to say in class. Kendall and I did an oral presentation on Albert Camus's book *The Stranger*. We received an A on our presentation – pissing off Dione because she received only a C for hers. She often bragged about how she was more proficient in French than us.

The French History classes were more difficult because we had no textbook to study from. Our professor would read from his one book and then expect us to memorize word for word what he had read out loud.

At the University of Poitiers there were no assignments or pop quizzes. In the history classes your grade depended upon how well you did on the final exam at the end of class – no grade or textbooks to study from, only your memory of your notes to rely on. In the literature classes, your grade depended upon your participation in class discussions as well as oral presentation and the final exam at the end of class. Reading from your assigned books was your homework.

During leisure time from schooling the Oregon students attended dance parties with French and other foreign students. French student Yvette danced with me and my Belgium-born friend Bruno, a SOSC student. After the dance Yvette invited us to her place. She had no real interest in him, neither friendship nor as a potential lover. I was her focus of interest because she was a lesbian. In reminiscing I thought maybe my first lover could have been a woman. I could be mistaken. For sure, Yvette and I didn't have a fling.

Another Oregon student had a party at his place. Gary was a musician I had a crush on, but his girlfriend (whom he met in France) was an Oregon student. He made a cassette tape of his composed songs that year and gave me a copy. While at the party, I had my first overseas asthma attack and I used an EpiPen of epinephrine to rescue me. My other medications didn't control the asthma affects.

At the time, I believed Gary's apartment was contaminated with mold, which most likely caused my asthma attack. He joked about it later, saying he had never had that kind of effect on anyone before. Wherever you are, Gary, I hope you're not sneezing too much in your current domain. Mold might be the culprit.

My itinerary included other European countries. I traveled alone to Brussels, Belgium, on a kind of literal hat trick: blindly selecting a single scrap of paper among many others out of a hat. My companions Kendall and Dione had written on them the names of various countries.

Brussels… where I met my first lover, Matthew, who was traveling with Beatrice, another American student. All along the way we visited fascinating castles. After Matthew and I became better acquainted and discovered we had more things in common than not, I decided I liked him very much.

Days later, on a moonlit night Vincent Van Gogh would have appreciated painting, we walked toward a secluded park area. Beatrice was elsewhere, thus providing us some privacy. We mostly exchanged passionate kisses until we became breathless. I had to warn that I didn't want to engage in sexual intercourse because I had left my diaphragm in France and I wanted to practice safe sex.

The next day, Matthew eagerly searched for available condoms and bought a pack at a near-by drug store. Later that day, we had our first sexual encounter. Seemed as though a miracle had happened and I received a badge of honor for holding out so long. Was I happy to end my virginity? I had mixed emotions that day, especially when Matthew – smiling hopefully through the window of the bus – waved good-bye to me. He took from me what I could never reclaim. What could have been a hot romance was only a one-night stand. That night, I wrote this poem for Matthew:

> The sea can no more hold the land,
> than the land can hold the sea.
> Bangor, a beach of stone.
>
> A dog patters towards me...
> We watch the birds dipping their
> beaks through beads of glass, until
> his owner calls him back.
>
> I stay by the shoreline... the dog looks
> again—his eyes are the birds, now
> bobbing like boats.
>
> I carried your parting look, numb to
> the weight of it, until a wall of sand
> began to break against my back.

> Those words I said just once, were
> liquid as the glass you stood behind,
> the bus stretching between us the
> distance of a dream.

I returned to France and my studies while Matthew and Beatrice continued traveling until they returned to Poitiers. Kendall and Dione took Beatrice on a tour of the city so that Matthew and I could have some time alone. We had sex for the second time but he prematurely climaxed. He was embarrassed by his own eagerness (lack of self-control, really) and apologized about not having more time to spend together. On his part, had absence from me increased the odds of us not having a *two*-hour bedroom session? I guess that didn't matter; I was so happy to see him and to feel his embrace.

Later that winter of 1984, I visited him and Beatrice in Bradford, England where they were studying English abroad. Matthew was a Philosophy major in Chico, California. Also a poet, he wrote a poem for me which was deeply touching. I stayed with him while I was in Bradford and we enjoyed sex for a third time. Our togetherness inspired me to write this poem:

Echo of Light

1.
Before colors, morning unspoken
but for birds whose wingtips
pluck a harp inside my head,
carry the wind as melody
disharmonic to ears behind eyes,
you pierce through in thick lines
dots suspended on a bubble of sleep.
Without dreams, now, I wake too early,
wanting rest as blackness still winds
itself blind to dawn.

2.
Then in gray day break, I'm etching
through tones disappearing beyond
white paper: I have pressed too hard,
made holes behind lids.
I felt your eyes moving in sleep
blue lit up underneath.
I loosened hands extending lightly
across your face—each finger plucked
from a doorknob, child-sized.

3.
In light, you threw my hands away
like scattering leaves in Winter, brittle
as my knees that crunched against a
carpet of my youth.
You dragged on clothes, as I followed
behind, a child again head bumping
down a hall.
I can no longer hear that day:
It is a deafening echo of light,
erasing me.

Betrayal? The truth about Matthew focused on him being an international playboy. He already was courting an English girlfriend named Tammy. He declared to me that they had not engaged in sex… merely lingering in bed with other English friends. His betrayal felt like a dagger had pierced my heart and sliced through my spine. In general, I'm not a violent person and very slow to burst into anger. But I imagined myself gouging his eyes out so he would never again appreciate admiring another's woman face and her vagina to screw. My friend Beatrice added injury to insult by saying – as if the statement was a back door put down – Matthew liked little women.

"Bony is more like it," I thought, after I met blue-eyed Tammy. I was petite, for sure, yet muscular from being an avid hiker and long distance runner.

Despairing about the betrayal of my first love affair but determined to keep my focus on my education, I left England and headed to Ireland. I decided to hitchhike to Dublin. I was fortunate enough to be picked up by a kind truck driver who said to me in his brogue accent, "You look like the Irish, my dear. Come along now." He told me all about his wife and little girls, missing them so much whenever he was away on his sojourns.

Upon arrival to Dublin, I immediately felt the thickness of the industrial smokiness of the air. I began coughing and experiencing shortness of breath. Compared to my aggravated condition, I saw citizens running down the street – as if they didn't have a care in the world. I wondered how they could tolerate such pollution entering their lungs.

I stayed in Dublin for only one day, as a youth hostel resident. I met another resident, an Australian woman who was also hitchhiking in Ireland. We decided to join forces and put out our thumbs. Soon, a lovely Irish woman driver picked us up and took us to Cork. My breathing faired no better in Cork because its atmosphere was equally polluted. Like a prisoner in a jail cell, I had to stay inside the youth hostel the whole time. I was wheezing without relief, preventing me from exploring the city.

The next day I started hitchhiking again, this time going to Northern Wales where the air was clean and fresh. I stayed in a Welsh youth hostel all by myself – this was in January 1984. I couldn't shake off my bad vibes about the creepiness of an overly curious male caretaker. The look in his eyes would have alarmed any young woman: a particular lust below the surface of his demeanor. His eyes were the color of hand-rubbed slate and they had a tendency to give my breasts too much attention in a sly way when he thought I wasn't looking. My intuition warned me to block the door with a chair, in case he decided to enter without an invitation.

My impression of Wales resembled the beautiful, verdant rolling hills of Ashland, Oregon (home of the internationally recognized Shakespearian Festival) but having an overcast characteristic like sister city Corvallis. After that first night in Wales, I hiked 15 miles to the next town. My backpack carried about 40 pounds of weight to help me improve my cardiovascular stamina; I would need it for long-distance running next spring. In the fall of 1983, I had been running six miles around Blosac Park in Poitiers or around the school track. Geraldine, my friend since first grade, ran with me but at a faster pace.

When the new spring season arrived, I found a country road to practice on my running; twice around the same route of about 13 miles… two to three times a week. The older men across the road would call out to me, *"Breathe through your nose!"*

Were they worried I would collapse and they'd have to render CPR? They didn't know about my medical history and why I had to breathe through my mouth while practicing running. That time was no exception because my nasal cavity was plugged from sinusitis. I didn't dare allow its wicked symptoms to defeat my passion for running.

By now, I was no longer running with Geraldine except for one time when I showed her my route. She was inspired to run on it too. She told me about the Paris Marathon the week before it was to occur, but she didn't give me any other information, perhaps assuming I already knew more information to pique my interest as a runner. Furthermore, she had a copy of *Runner's World* Magazine and didn't share it with me. I think she didn't want me to compete in the marathon, so that she could brag about how much better she was as a runner – *fiercely* competitive.

The week before the marathon I ran four times around my regular route (just to prove to myself that I was capable) which equaled 26 miles. In the middle of the week before the marathon, I tried to run but could only achieve 10 miles because my legs ached worse than a toothache. I spent the rest of the day resting and studying by the radiator where it was warm. I also painted an abstract with oils showing a woman's legs and head; the rest of her body was covered by swirls of blue and orange. Somehow, painting relaxed me whenever I was fatigued from many hours of focused studying.

* * *

After final exams, the concierge who worked for the law office (below my room in Poitiers) let me stay on through the rest of June. Then in July, Kendall and I went traveling, using our Interrail passes. We had $400 left over from the OSSHE study abroad program. Our destination was Greece. We went via Yugoslavia – traveling for three days on a crowded train where there wasn't enough vacant seats to sit in. So, we ended up sitting in the partitions between cars or standing looking out the window. At night we slept by the bathroom in our sleeping bags which had been rolled up beneath our backpacks.

On the train, we met a Yugoslavian man who didn't know English or French, but tried to speak to us in German, but we didn't speak his language. We communicated without spoken words, managing to share our wheat meal biscuits with him, and he shared his juice.

At last, we boarded the ferry to get to the Greek Islands. While aboard I contracted an ear infection. My companion Kendall was like a nurse, speaking in soothing tones to help ease the pain. After we stepped off the ferry in Athens, we rushed to the nearest hospital, where we waited a ridiculous three hours for emergency assistance from a doctor. It was all about order and first come first serve. Each at-risk patient had to tear a numbered ticket from a ticket machine in the lobby. For example, if your heart was literally beating *through* your chest, well… too bad for you. You'll still have to wait until a doctor gave another patient a checkup and write a prescription for horrendous bad breath.

The epic wait culminated in a curly haired, gaunt-faced doctor giving my achy ear a flushing and a prescription for antibiotic eardrops.

We ventured to Crete and lastly to a little island near Turkey, where even the tourist police had a hard time finding. With much reluctance, we rented a two-dollar-a-night motel room. With great ease, monster-like cockroaches scaled the outside walls of that motel. We made the mistake of hiding a bag of half-eaten fruit underneath the bed. I suppose the smell of early stage decaying fruit made their scent receptors go nuts because those cockroaches found ways to enter our less than appealing room.

I feared them like I feared the giant rats of New York City. I was all choked up inside and my clammy skin felt creepy-crawly. *Oh god! Would they hang around come bedtime?* That possibility sent chills down my spine. On the other hand, Kendall seemed fearless like a seasoned warrior who was ready to commit terminating violence against them. After all, she was born and raised in Guam. As a preteen – cute, leggy, inquisitive about everything and everybody – she chased them and smashed them with a removable shower pole. Now in adulthood, she managed to decimate at least half of the motel's cockroach tribe.

We vacationed on that mini-island for nearly two weeks. Unfiltered by overcast skies, the sun was brighter and casting hotter rays those days… the temperature was 120 degrees Fahrenheit but producing dry heat. During the mornings, we ate breakfasts of dense, thin bread and yogurt. Shopped for fruit at open-air markets. In the afternoons, we sunbathed, taking off our tops, but not our bottoms. In comparison, the Grecian people sunbathed naked.

I loved swimming in the ocean; the area I swam in was pale bluish-green and you could see large bone-white rocks below the surface. When I reached the blue water, farther out, I would turn because I could no longer see what was below me. Kendall had told me horror stories about sharks she had seen in Guam. I hoped she hadn't tried to eradicate any with a detached shower pole.

After our sojourn in Greece, we took a ferry to mainland Europe, taking a train to East Croydon, just outside London, England. On the train, we met two guys, one English, dark-haired Jerry, and one Irish, red-haired Michael. Eventually they accompanied us to our destination, showing us the way to the nearby YWCA. Something about their demeanors reminded me of slick street thugs who are good at charming unsuspecting women their ages. Easy money over potential sex would be the bottom line.

Once we had deposited our backpacks in the assigned room, we entered the kitchen and made dinner for four: plain lettuce and cheese. Michael, the tallest and muscular, regaled that our naked lettuce and cheese was a "lovely meal". He probably was more a meat and potatoes eater.

I didn't know anything about Jerry's background to encourage me enough to fully trust him. He was short and stocky and bow-legged. He often bragged about having an impressive "six-pack" of abs. Did he think his washboard abdominal area was a chick magnet? What he did next took me by surprise. He looked in the refrigerator's freezer compartment and withdrew a harmless chicken.

As if it were a soccer ball, he tossed the future dinner in the air several times before yelling, "Fly free, chickee, fly free!" Under normal circumstances, chickens don't fly. But this one did when he marched to the window and threw it out of the second story window. I still don't know why he protested to that level. Perhaps he was one of those animal rights advocates. Perhaps he was a secret Green Peace member. Keen on animal rights.

After that performance, they invited themselves to our designated room and spent the night.

Early the next morning, the likable rogues escaped out the window and down the fire escape. We never saw them again.

Our breakfast was diverse: Kendall had baked beans and red wine; I had bran cereal with milk. Soon, the mannish, linebacker of a housekeeper came to our room. Her scowl of disapproval was wider than a Texas landscape. She thrust a well-worn bible into my chest, pursed her lips harder before she exited. The air was full of her religious conformist attitude. We weren't intimidated. We speculated that she knew that two derelict guys had shacked up with us.

Our next stop was Shrewsberry, England. Kendall had an English boyfriend who she had met in France. He lived there with his parents. The English was very gracious, but the industrial smog was thick in the air and all I could think about was trying to breathe; I was wheezing the whole time I was a guest. After a two-day stay we headed to Paris, France where I said "good-bye" to Kendall at the airport. She was returning home in America.

On the train to Paris, I met three Icelandic guys who "adopted" me as a traveling companion since I spoke French well. We all went out to dinner and drank lots of red wine. I was tipsy because of my low tolerance for alcoholic beverages. One thing led to another and we decided to rent a motel room, preferably with two beds.

    I can imagine your justified criticism over my risky adventures with male strangers abroad… putting my life in danger each time – from crippling venereal diseases to rape to murder. I suppose luck, as if a protective shield, was in my corner. I suppose I was too trusting again because I had a wild time with two of the guys; the third guy stayed to himself on the second bed. The next night, I stayed in the room with just one of the Icelandic guys, Erik. We had a great, lovely time together. Later he would become a long-distance boyfriend. I wrote this poem for him about that second night, alone with him in Paris:

> I smiled into your shoulder,
> slept deeply remembering our
> caress of feet as we lay together.
>
> That simple touching hummed
> even in our first meeting: the corridor
> of a crowded train Paris, my last
> time headed there, your first.
>
> In the morning as we lingered in
> rumpled white, my glance came
> gliding along your back – tasting
> of your salt – as if your were a beach,
> remnant of my breath.
>
> Just before I left, your eyes were as a
> vast Icelandic winter whose days fall
>
> soft through flashing lights.
> You'd touch my soul as if I were a
> wild thing amidst the snow.
> Two seeds, we'd emptied our hearts
> to August-thick air: ruddy apples just

beginning to drop.

> Now, across these waters, I see your
> in the leaves, golden and brown, they drift
> across my face.
> Now, I reach out, touch cedar: your breath
> is there as a memory in soft-jointed green.

Just like in the movies, where two potential lovers are forced apart by circumstances not under their control. Tears and promises. Those deeply sincere, can't wait to see you again expressions. A final departing hug feeling ultra-wonderful and maybe a lingering good-bye kiss... while other ticketed plane passengers – some smiling, some hopeful, others more focused on their own particular fates – watch with curious eyes. *Oh my. Love birds so much in love*, a few might say to themselves.

Nope. No transitional romantic scene like that between Erik and me because for personal reasons he was unable to escort me to insanely busy Charles de Gaulle Airport. (Even there his inoffensive musty scent clung to parts of my body he had aroused.) I had no reason not to disbelieve why he couldn't accompany me. Still, the ache of departure from him and Paris left me in a bittersweet mood while I waited in a leather armchair for my 10 am flight back to America, specifically Corvallis, Oregon where my parents lived. Earlier, I had phoned them and they seemed happy – genuinely *relieved* – to hear my voice and thankful that I would be returning soon.

The eighteen-hour flight was uneventful, with the exception of a young mother's toddler crying that was too much annoyance for irked passengers. All I thought about for a while was my budding relationship with Eric and how the chemistry between us seemed so right, so special. I wanted him to be the father of our first child... maybe two. I wondered if my parents would like him enough to accept him into my family? And would his Icelandic parents reciprocate?

By the time my father picked me up at Portland International Airport, my jet lag felt like a compressor was already crushing my mind and body toward a strange fatigue. Departing planes roaring off. Other motorists determined to pick up curbside passengers. Traffic security teams blowing their whistles. Utility pole lights. Chatter of walking citizens trying to escape from the 1am luggage stampede... all of that business gave me a heightened sensation of reality, as if I were deep under water and it was about ready to implode between my ears.

When my father guided his trusty pickup onto Interstate 5 Southbound he gave me a worried glance. "You gonna be okay, honey?"

If I didn't look haggard, I felt like it. Maybe looking several years older: new haircut turned straggly, dark circles below eyes that telegraphed a grumpy attitude. My heavy, stuffy head was pressed against the passenger side window. The image resembled a victim of a broken neck. Certainly I couldn't share with him the loads of crazy sex I had enjoyed with various young men abroad. Eric was Number One among them all.

I mumbled, "Nothing to be concerned about, Dad. I'll get through it."

"Did you have a serious asthma attack at any time?" He glanced at me again before he changed to the fast left lane. He was traveling over 65 mph.

My eyes were closed. I barely raised two fingers. "Only twice." I was too drained to offer full-blown details. He must have sensed I wasn't ready for a lengthy conversation while in route. We maintained a respectful silence during the remaining miles.

July turned into August. I had arrived back in time to participate in my cousin Brenda's wedding. I remember the plaid blue, maroon and sea green dress with a ruffle at the hem I wore to her wedding – my mom had picked it out. I was very tan due to sunbathing in Greece. I had a new haircut crafted in Paris, making my hair flow down past my shoulders. It was one of the most photogenic pictures ever of me. I looked healthy and rested. A certain peace existed in my soul.

Her first wedding was beautiful in all the traditional ways, but her marriage eventually ended in a messy divorce. From that failure, she married again... this time to a *woman*. Goes to show you how fate can make decisions for us and guide our lives in different directions.

After staying a couple weeks in Corvallis, I transferred from SOSC to the University of Oregon, in Eugene. My first year there I lived in a studio apartment. I had neither a phone nor much contact (except in classes) with most of my friends from the OSSHE overseas program, though it seemed that the ones who had attended SOSC prior to going to France had also transferred to the U of O. Roger was a neighbor who owned a St. Bernard named Breaker. Breaker's curiosity lead him to visit me on the first floor of the apartment building; Roger lived on the second floor. We ended up having a brief affair. He was kind of kooky... ate hallucinogenic mushrooms and gave poor Breaker portions.

I kept in touch with my first lover Matthew who resided in Chico, California, via letters. During this letter writing campaign period, I hitchhiked a ride down to Chico with a perverted sex offender Religion professor. (I didn't find out the truth until a week later, after the ride to Chico and back.) He had been molesting his young daughter for years. He was finally sentenced to 25 years in prison.

I wrote to Matthew and asked if I could come visit him before I headed to Chico. He said that would be cool because he recently ended his relationship with his twiggy English girlfriend. She was a visitor at his place for a month then returned to England.

When I got to Chico, Matthew tried to pawn me off on his neighbors. He thought he was slick, by not wanting me to cohabitate with him at his apartment because he had started a new relationship with Margot, another student in Chico. I wasn't a pushover who was desperate for male attention, especially of the sexual kind. So I refused to stay with strangers and slept on a separate mattress rather than Matthew's bed. But one night, I approached him and we almost made love. My nervousness prevented me from kissing him back, thus turning off his desire.

He wrote me a poem about a butterfly-ballerina (meaning me) that had been in his love-light only briefly, and now was dying. Compared to me, Margot was pleasant, round-hipped, with beautiful dark brown naturally curly hair and rosy cheeks. I liked her but I was kind of mixed up crazy, spending most of the week alone – at Matthew's request because he wanted to be with Margot. I still remember the Ricki Lee

Jones cassette tape that he played, as well as the Ramen noodles each of us often ate for dinner. It felt basically like another rejection, but why shouldn't he have a girlfriend who lived near to him, in Chico?

Hank was another man that I had had a crush on at SOSC. He had also transferred to the U of O that first year I was back from Europe. We had corresponded while I was in France. Beyond my crush on him, we became good friends. He was also an English major; we had classes together. I was happy for him when he found a woman that I knew. She became the perfect match for him because of his manliness. She had grown up with all brothers, so she understood Hank's personality and quirks.

She was in my choreography dance class and did an impromptu dance for class. We were all required to make up our own solo dance to do for the class. I performed a routine to the Jonathan Livingston Seagull record with the song *Be*.

At the end of the dance, I stood balancing on one foot with my toes raised as far as they could stretch, like a ballerina in her toe shoes. My one leg was bent at the knee while touching the side of my other knee and my arms were asymmetrically balanced with one arm straight up and the other straight out from my body. For my athleticism, I received applause from the other students and instructor. That kind of recognition made me happy throughout the day.

I was happier for Hank and his soul mate Margot who he later married. I attended their wedding reception. Before I traveled to France, I wrote the following poem for Hank who was a river guide:

> Do you remember
> those moments
> when you wanted
> to hold the world
> away from yourself?
>
> A harmonica plays
> catching the gaze
> of the sun

through an open window.

You are the dust
carried by the sun
where your Pegasus—
ramble of mind
seeks a voice outdoors.

But your wing gets caught
in dry branches
and you swirl to the river
in a backlog of birdsong,
sharp and frantic to fill
that dying hush of Winter
with Spring.

The river rambling away
and a way, continues the dream.

In my fifth year in college – my first year at U of O, I changed my major to French because I had more French credits than English. I studied in the final year (1985-86) at the university while I worked three full-time jobs: at the university's Science Library, the cafeteria, and biking to a nursing home four days a week (working the 3 pm to 11 pm shift and sometimes staying over for the night shift). I liked the residents there and would spend time talking with each one, but a nurse's work review report revealed that "... *I spent too much time socializing with the residents...*" What a slap in the face for my being empathetic and showing concern for their mental and physical health!

Feeling more sorry for those residents than myself, I abruptly quit because I refused to be a cold and emotionally distant robot in that environment.

* * *

I now lived in a boarding house for women above a popular Chinese restaurant. Each of the seven other women had her own room. We were like a family of modern-day hippies without serious political agendas, even though the state of the world was in political chaos.

I became friends with a colorful lesbian couple; the more aggressive one of the pair always bummed off my homemade yogurt as a curative agent to help her incessant yeast infections. My curiosity about her typical female problem prodded me to do a little research. I discovered that Greek yogurt contains good bacteria that doesn't promote yeast activity in the vagina, especially when said yogurt is neither sweetened nor flavored sweetened.

The yeast feeds on such sugars and worsens the infection. I must admit I used a few blended banana slices in my homemade yogurt but they shouldn't have promoted yeast growth in Tamara's vagina. What still puzzles me today is why she didn't decide to make her own dog-gone yogurt concoction and not rely on my supply? Heck, you couldn't get any cheaper than homemade!

Another colorful tenant was a Vietnamese woman named Bui (BOO-EE). She barely towered over five feet and probably weighed only 80 pounds. Below jet black short hair was her best facial feature: almond-shaped brown eyes that carried a soulful depth. Oh what a voice in a small human package! She could hit those high notes of her favorite songs.

On one particular Saturday night around 8 pm, while all the other tenants were absent, she ventured to her favorite makeshift stage… the rooftop outside her window. I'm still amazed none of the restaurant customers complained about her free spiritedness.

I was inspired to see her in action again and maybe sing along with her.

When Bui saw me approach, she stopped singing the lyrics of the mega hit single "Respect". In 1967, R&B singer Aretha Franklin had turned that song into a wake-up call for women's rights and protest about equality for women, globally. However, R&B soul singer Otis Redding was the *original* writer and producer of the song in 1965 and had a different targeted theme not focused on women's rights. The beat was so funky and provocative you couldn't help but shake your tail feathers while dancing.

"You like song, Zae?" Bui asked, smiling like an impish child.

I looked down into her liquid eyes. "Very much." The truth was that I had heard "Respect" only twice on a boyfriend's car radio while we were making out on an abandoned country road.

I glanced about and saw the evening's last highlights of dusk only minutes away from vanishing. Early summertime stars would blanket the sky next.

"I know all words; no problem. You?"

"Wish I did."

"No problem; I show you." Bui withdrew a folded sheet of paper from the rear pocket of her cut-off jeans. She had typewritten the lyrics. Together we read the words several times before we tried our first duet. Took several tries before our different voices blended in better. Afterward, we thrust our fists up at the stars and yelled "MORE POWER TO WOMEN LIKE US!!" We must have laughed until our rib cages ached.

Bui had a roommate who shared the one room with her. She was Sarah, Nordic tall and buxom. Bui adored her but otherwise they were a mismatch. Fun loving Gail was another tenant whose sexy hazel eyes and olive complexion never failed to make me a little envious of her photogenic face. Her sandy colored hair always looked like wayward corkscrews. She allowed her black boyfriend, a Duck basketball athlete, to shack up with her almost every night.

Besides Bui, I befriended Sharon, the other lesbian partner who didn't suffer from constant yeast infections. I met a few guys that year too. I had a fling with a super-smart Korean who was deep into computer programming. Maybe that's why our affair blew out its four tires: he was more advanced in computer knowledge than me. Hearing him talk about it gave me tension headaches.

Sometimes, we don't have control over the people who like us *first* and appreciate qualities they see in us after a first impression. For example, I had a hiking buddy named Roy. Initially we were complete strangers. He was a tall, skinny, and pimply-faced jogger. When we first met at a Eugene park near campus, he said he could tell by my flat stomach that I was a serious runner. That day, I wore a navy blue tank top, white gym shorts, and feet tucked into well-worn Nike running shoes. He correctly assumed that I was dedicated to my passion and much disciplined... even down to my diet. We had a short-lived fling because his true interest was directed at a flirtatious, bubble-butt Asian woman in our hiking club. Oh well... I suppose white girls with irresistible charms can be rejected too.

My other buddy was Bruno. We couldn't wait to attend ball room dancing events, preferably my cup of tea. No pun intended, but we always had a... ball whenever we polished the floors with the soles of our shoes. Dress up like celebrities. Smell like a spring garden in Pasadena. He originally went to SOSC and to France, where we became companions. He also transferred to U of O. He was born in Belgium. His Belgium parents migrated to the U.S. and became citizens. He grew up mostly under the parental authority of his mother; from the early stages of his birth, and beyond, his dad was an absentee mystery.

Bruno's mother was a talented writer and free-spirited. Yet, he often felt insecure around other women who he felt an attraction to, because of his short stature, prematurely balding head, and natural gruffness in his voice. I didn't dismiss his uniqueness and open-mindedness. His social activities were diverse: from ballroom dancing to archery competition.

Eventually, Bruno traveled to Japan, learned the language, and fell head over heels in love with a brunette-haired English woman who spoke fluent Japanese. In a lengthy December letter, he told me she nicknamed him "Bruns".

There's a saying I learned long ago when it comes to women-men relationships dealing with intimacy. No one woman or man can fulfill all of your wants but *needs* stand a much better chance of being fulfilled. You'd think high-profile celebrities, lawyers, politicians, sports personalities, and zillionaires would have no problem finding and keeping a worthy companion they would later marry and have kids with, and march step by step toward a bright future... only to file for divorce a few years later. Happens all the time, even among the best of us.

So, there were two other (*hint*) Asian guys I met and each aroused my curiosity. Wen Ping and his other countryman went by the American name Paul. I tutored Wen Ping in writing English. I invited him out to go dancing with me. He was the shyest person I ever met, and his feet coordination wasn't up to par. Remember that extremely popular 1970s TV dance show *Soul Train,* where cool-looking, fashionably dressed African-American teens danced to the latest hit songs and be entertained by the hottest soul singers – live on the set – of R&B royalty? And the ever too cool host Don Cornelius with the sexy bass voice? It's a good thing Wen Ping was not of that era and on that stage. I think you get my point. From the beginning, I didn't have any high hopes of getting better acquainted with him. A potential friendship went nowhere.

I met alias Paul, originally from Singapore and an English major, through our mutual cafeteria job. I truly liked him because he wasn't prejudiced against white people, had an overall positive outlook on life, and was ambitious enough to want to make a difference in the world. Plus, he was cute like the martial arts genius (Kung Fu, in particular) and heartthrob Bruce Lee.

Paul accepted my invitation to my END OF THE SCHOOL YEAR PARTY, before I'd travel to New York City that summer to live with my sister and her boyfriend. Like me, he suffered from asthma and had an attack at my party. He had his medication with him; yet, I also had to massage his back to substantially relax those muscles which cramp up when you have difficulty breathing. He said to me, before he left the party, that if I was coming back in the fall that he would make an authentic, traditional Chinese dinner for us. Good intentions? You bet he did. But even expensive clothes fade when they get too much direct sun over a lengthy time.

I thought that I would only stay the summer in NYC and come back to get a second major in International Studies, but that is not what happened.

CHAPTER SIX

AND THE DOUBLE BEAT GOES ON

July Fourth, Independence Day 1986... New York City.

That day I was seated in a taxi with my sister and heading to her upper west side apartment. The first thing I noticed in the Big Apple was the *boom-boom-boom* noises that were going off all around me. Having only seen the bustling city in famous movies, I assumed that they were just expected gunshots, and that people nearby were trying to kill each other. Later, I realized the commotion was attributed to celebration fireworks.

Finally, we arrived in the neighborhood that was considered Hispanic Harlem. The residents were mostly Puerto Rican or African American. I was a minority here and I started to empathize with others who were considered minorities in my small part of the world – cities of Oregon: Corvallis, Ashland, Eugene.

I started working within the first three days of my arrival. I took a typing test, and my speed was 67 words per minute without errors. All of my English papers that I wrote in college paid off. I was hired as a typist through a temporary employment agency. I couldn't believe how easy it was to get a job. My first temp job was at Hilton International. My fluency in speaking French was a valuable asset too. I met my first friend who lived in New Jersey. Clarissa also was fluent in French which we often conversed in.

On the weekends, we would go out to eat. I still remember the white pizza (without tomato sauce) that we ate… truly scrumptious. My sister, Tess, introduced me to two of her friends, Sari and Haviar, who had a beautiful girl of Finnish and Peruvian ancestry. Tess, Sari, Crystal and I went to Central Park and danced to live music. Years later, when I reflected back on that day and another day of dancing in Portland, Oregon, I wrote this poem:

Dancing of Necessity

In fading light they sit and talk of lifetimes that hurt
and hurt beyond hurt, and still she held his hand and
gently said, "Sweetie, I think you need to wipe this
corner of your mouth."

Sunlight overturning leaves in breeze, she says,
"Just going up to the roof to do my daily writing,
keep in practice."

Stream of consciousness, like the apple,
only half-eaten, that the roach left his germs on.

New York City haze on nylons, Heat and noise,
then, in park, a new world, slowed baby Crystal
on mother, Sari's hip, dancing.

We are all dancing, me, my sister, Sari, Crystal,
dancing alone yet together, like a breezy flute,
jazz beat not expectantly fluid, yet fluid beyond
air currents brought to your limbs from your core.
Dancing of necessity, brings us closer to just being
fully alive.

She stomps her feet to the woman's song in the
karaoke bar, and refuses to follow a man's lead,

or to take his hand and go to the center of the group,
squished, unable to move her feet freely.
He's drunk and keeps coaxing her, but she says,
"No, I don't want to," and "No, I'll smile if I
want to. I'm a very independent woman!"

Another time I went to a jazz concert with Sari and Haviar. They lived in Long Island and had hired a babysitter for the night. We went out to eat after the concert and I had an asthma attack. We boarded a subway train and returned to my sister's apartment. Somehow, I had forgotten to bring my inhaler. Sari did a good job of soothing me, rubbing my back to release the tension which otherwise would exacerbate the asthma. She and Haviar were very relieved when I resumed breathing normally again.

In the two and a half years I ended up living with Tess and Rafi, I had temp jobs that lasted for six months each at US Sprint and Tiffany's. Then I also worked part-time for Lincoln Center for the Performing Arts as a telemarketer, and another part-time position at the Natural History Museum as a receptionist and a Saturday job as a legal typist for an immigration lawyer. Later, I worked at Columbia University's Geology library as a Level 5 library clerk.

I alone oversaw the library three days a week. I remember how peaceful the area was when I was in control. However, strong personality conflicts existed between me and the senior librarian. That's why my probationary period lasted only three months. If I had been granted a permanent status, I had planned to take six free credits per term to earn my master's degree in library science.

Through chitchats I made attempts to become more familiar with the senior librarian, but after I told her that my sister had a Dominican boyfriend, her attitude changed towards me... she became cold, distant, patronizing, and complained about minorities taking unfair advantage of overly liberal social programs like welfare payments and food stamps. It would be easy to say she was a racist, but I was convinced she was at least prejudice against citizens of color.

In August of 1986, I traveled from NYC to ReyKavik, Iceland. I stayed with Erik, his parents, and younger brother and sister. Erik's current construction job prevented us from spending more free time together. On weekends, I met his other Icelandic friends and we partied together. One night, while his friends were quickly becoming my friends, I got separated from Erik – he went home without me. His friends were graciously protective of me and made sure I returned to Erik's home, safely. I was surprised by such caring. I didn't know many Americans who would do the same with a stranger. I appreciated Linda's and Drifa's acceptance of me as Erik's American girlfriend.

At Linda's house, I remember eating parts of a lamb – brain, kidney and liver were specialties. I liked the kidney the best. Icelandic farmers bred larger lambs, thus larger organs. The liver was cooked like a juicy beefsteak.

Teen sister Jona and I would watch movies. Known as soccer in the U.S., I attended her and her younger brother's football games. With her help I wrote in Icelandic language a story called "The Idiot" (a supernatural tale about a male statue that comes alive and – like a wakeup call – causes great havoc.)

I did some cleaning for Erik's mother while she worked full-time at a bakery. His father worked in the construction industry, once owning his own construction company. Starting at age 15, Erik had worked for his father and now Eric knew how to build a house from the ground up. He had only a fifth grade education but school there was more advanced than in the U.S. I read one of his school papers, written in English, about a Steinbeck novel and the writing critique was better than the college students I had tutored in the Writing Lab at SOSC.

One summer Erik and I walked through picturesque meadows and bathed in the hot springs. Icelandic homes were run by geothermal heat. The air smelled fresh and clean – a wonderful reality that refreshed me when I engaged in running. Even serious crime was shockingly low.

One weekend we went camping and there was a platform out in the country where a band played at night. Many Icelandic youth, including my new friends and I, drank and danced until the wee hours. Too much drinking dehydrated me and triggered an asthma attack. I stayed the rest of the night in the tent. Although I used my inhaler frequently, I still had difficulty breathing.

I survived to see the next morning and I restored my hydration with only water, and my sobriety. I later became irritated about how slow the music attendees were packing up to leave. I came to realize that Icelandic culture was vastly different... moved at a slower pace, less hectic and crowded – light years away from being a New York City.

When it was time for me to fly back to America, I remembered Erik hugging me tighter than usual in the living room. To me, that felt like a good sign – not so much as a gesture of possession but of impending loss of my physical presence, of how I looked and smelled. We were alone that overcast and drizzly Friday afternoon around two. His siblings were still in school and his mother had remaining hours of work at the bakery.

Before he kissed me, he said, "Zae, I love you like grass sucks in rain. The long distance between us will become history in our story." His hands slid down to my rear and massaged it. We had had sex the previous night at one of his friend's spare bedrooms. But it was too late to crave for more.

"I'm not ready to leave you behind," I said, after our lips separated.

"That won't matter because I will be thinking about you every minute, as if you never left."

I looked deeper into his eyes and felt nothing but genuine honesty. I had no doubt about wanting to spend the rest of my life with him as my future husband. "We're facing a long road ahead, sir." I smiled with confidence, but I hid my inner fears from him. "Time, as you know, changes things *and* people."

Erik nodded. "Oh sure. Time, also, is a healer, a gage to test the strength of commitment." He chuckled. "Only quitters lose at the game."

A moment of intense silence was broken by my response.

"Quitters may lose at the game, but doing so sometimes destroys lives."

My future husband shrugged and grinned.

Another shroud of silence fell over us while we traveled to the airport.

Later in June 1987, I traveled from NYC to a little town just outside Bordeaux, France. I had procured a job through one of my sister's high school friends who had married the French brother of a family who needed an au pair (nanny) for the summer. The French kids I nannied consisted of three girls (Greta–ten; Manuela–eight; Sada–five) and a one-year-old boy named Hugo.

Besides looking after the kids, mostly Hugo, I did housework. I escaped from cooking duties, though, when I said to Eva Magnusson, the stay-at-home mother, "All I know how to cook well is rice, beans, and vegetables. I've been a vegetarian for years. Sorry, ma'am."

The father was Dr. Biork Magnusson, an endocrinologist who was handsomely gray-haired, squared-jaw, and showed a sly grin whenever he got a point across to a listener. (He would return home to make lunch for us and then return to his office within walking distance.) He was more patient and understanding than his post-menopausal wife. Tall, thin, and easily agitated, she had directed past au pairs to also perform duties of a housewife so she could spend more time doing other activities: conducting catechism classes, in particular. Inwardly, I disagreed with Eva when she criticized about Americans spending too much time fussing over their children and warned me not to spend too much time with baby Hugo. When I ended my duties he would be staying behind his child's gate, playing by himself. It was easy for me to love him.

His sister Manuela, precocious at eight, said to me one day, "You are plenty good with him. You treat him like he is your *own* son!" That was one of my proudest moments in France.

I was given one day off from work. I used that free time for three-hour walks in the countryside. One particular workday I had an asthma attack while I was bathing baby Hugo. I pleaded with her to allow me to swap the work day… return the next day when I'd feel normal. She acted like a cold-blooded bitch. She expressed only contempt about my breathing difficulty and still expected me to do laundry and iron Hugo's baby clothes on a *mini-ironing* board!

Like a TV show wrestling ring judge, Dr. Magnusson intervened during his lunch hour. After he quieted his agitated wife, he gave me cortisone medicine and dismissed me from remaining work time. I promised him I would show up earlier the next day. His kindness to me will never be forgotten.

At summer's end, I was due to return to the Big Apple. I was facing significant travel fatigue. I saw a short cut. I asked the Magnussons if they could make it less stressful on me by buying me a ticket via Iceland; that option would return me faster to my temporary home. They agreed, but I felt I didn't have the full blessings of bitchy Eva. The ticket enabled me to visit Erik in Iceland for a couple weeks. Somehow, he thought I was coming later; that's why he didn't meet me at the airport. I traveled by bus to my friend Linda's house and spent a week with her and her mom and three other daughters.

During late fall of that same year, my Paris friend Finnbogi and his nerdy girlfriend Shelly came to visit me in New York City. She actually had a big head that was a mismatch to her juvenile looking body. Because she was naturally smarter than us all, her I.Q. was rumored to be off the calculation chart. Her brain got her acceptance to study for her master's degree in chemistry at the University of Michigan.

In my tiny kitchen, we were watching a pot of corn segments boiling. I remember she instructed me to "cook ze corn on ze cob longer – please do – until it turns soggy... yes?"

Did nerdy Shelly wear false teeth? I wasn't a big corn eater but I didn't like it Shelly's way – *mushy*. Creamy Corn du jour, anybody?

Here's another oddity about the couple. I had bought groceries for the three of us, but every morning Finnbogi (a bearded, teddy bear who was charming but socially awkward) and Shelly went to McDonald's for breakfast. They behaved as if eating there was a fetish. Even when we went one night to eat in Greenwich Village, they insisted we go to McDonald's instead. I don't believe economic shortcomings played a role in their consumer loyalty. So I entered a next-door deli where the proprietor had an excellent salad bar. I purchased a Greek salad, grabbed packets of salad dressing, and carried the stuff back into McDonald's.

In astonishment, they stared at the offering, then stared at me.

I stared back, puzzled.

Almost in unison, they said, "No,no,no. You buy salad here – McDonald's."

I stared harder, trying my best to show some degree of diplomacy.

"Look, you guys... *I don't like McDonald's plain iceberg lettuce salad. OK?*"

They brooded until they sampled the Greek salad. For my honesty they fought back with several hours of more silence back at my apartment.

From October to December 1988, Erik came to NYC to live with me, my sister, and her boyfriend. At that time, I was an entry-level editorial assistant for Elsevier Publishing Company and worked under an editor named Jane. The Dutch-owned company specialized in scientific, technical, and medical content. I liked my duties and responsibilities and envisioned myself climbing up the ladder toward better pay, and positions of power and authority. I was game for permanent employment until Erik asked me to marry him (not a second worth of hesitation from me!) while we were heading for Seattle, Washington, in January 1989. We lived there with my brother for three months until Erik's visa expired, and he went back to Iceland to obtain his fiancée visa.

From the beginning of Erik's visit with us in America, his personality reflected his nature of being the life of the party – funny, joking, even more pumped up whenever he drank alcohol responsibly. And having a take charge/follow me/you'll be glad you did mindset. He was straightforward with my sister and her boyfriend. Their chemistry made our living together less stressful and hounded less by domestic conflicts. He shared in the expenses, housekeeping duties, and cooked appetizing meals.

He loved the drizzly days that had descended upon Central Park, where we would take weekend walks, protected by rain gear. He had a thing for eating ice cream in cones, drinking soda from a straw or tossing Gummy Bears into the air and allowing his opened mouth to catch them; enjoyed doing the act on the subways too – made a contest out of it. We explored old record shops and bookstores. We saw two Off-Off Broadway shows whose themes made us have lively discussions about the inherent hazards of married couples having an open marriage.

We both wanted a maximum of three children but we couldn't decide at what point in time would be most beneficial to start a family.

Then, like the unexpected bombshell cliché, came the multi-headed monster of rejection, loss, and heartbreak.

It was July 1989 that I had my wedding planned for – scheduled to happen in Corvallis, Oregon… under the gazebo in Central Park (not NYC's) with the reception at my church. I invited about 50 guests, and I was going to make a homemade cheesecake with tofu instead of eggs (causing allergic reactions in me) in lieu of a traditional wedding cake. I had planned to have my friend Gary play his Spanish guitar at my wedding. However, I head from my Icelandic friend, Linda, that Erik was with a Norwegian by then, someone he had met at the fish factory where he was working. He didn't even bother telling me, so I canceled all the wedding plans. I had had high hopes from the beginning about Erik and I regarding marriage. I suppose that fate wasn't meant to happen. He wasn't seriously ready for that kind of "until death screws us apart" commitment.

After the wedding debacle, I planned to move to Portland, Oregon. Initially, I stayed with some friends, Kendall and her boyfriend Dennis, who lived in Tualatin – a bus ride away from downtown Portland, where I looked for an apartment to rent and a job. I tried the temporary agencies first but didn't find a job until I applied at Camera World. I found a one-bedroom apartment in downtown – within walking distance of my new job as a Camera World clerk. Working there would change my life and give me a newfound sense of hope in the realm of lasting love. I couldn't afford to fail again.

CHAPTER SEVEN

MARRIAGE MERRY-GO ROUND

We humans have the capacity to grieve over numerous circumstances in our lives but grief effects each of us differently. A fifty-year marriage between a dedicated couple, for example, ends when the opposite spouse partner dies from a terminal disease. The loss is incalculable and irreplaceable. The survivor's world is shattered to the point that living alone isn't sustainable, even though nearby or distant relatives are available to offer moral support and comfort. Yet, a strong focus on the loss predicament causes the survivor to swirl further into a black hole of depression, misery, and self-imposed guilt. Sooner or later, the survivor dies from the complexities of grief.

I thought I was capable of not allowing myself to "go under" a similar black hole of grief over the failure of Erik's last minute decision not to marry me just because he wanted to share his life with another woman I didn't know. I suppose love is like a drug and apparently I couldn't get enough of Erik's. He had filled a facet of my life with his love, affection, reliability, respect, and humor – until the figurative bombshell of deceit exploded in my mind. What was it about me that he was driven to flip the script and be motivated enough to reject *everything* about me, as if he were playing a role in a video game and he could change the rules of engagement at the slightest whim? Would he have behaved the same ruthless way if later he found me to be undesirable across the board, thus pumping up his confidence to ask me for a divorce? A commitment to marriage is a FULL TIME JOB not meant to be taken for granted. One thing I'm grateful for, however, is that his decision spared us the various future costs (not all in monetary terms) associated with a divorce. A point to reflect on, especially these days: some nasty divorces end in suicide or homicide or both at the same time.

I had shared my heartbreak with family members who offered moral support and encouraged me to move forward and to stay positive. My girlfriends offered hugs, drinks, and a spirit of camaraderie. They even bad-mouthed Erik as if he were a cyclopean monster dug up from a toxic lagoon where ten thousand bodies of other women like me were buried.

Still, all of that wonderful cheer leading didn't diminish my grief over Erik. It was a 24-hour shadow invader with a life of its own. It chased me in dreams about Erik. It taunted me whenever I watched romantic comedies on TV. Later, it forced me to take a wrong left turn towards a kind of self-destructive behavior: over-feeding myself.

I always had a good appetite and ate sensibly. Erik was going to marry a physically fit bride, minus the complications of having asthma… that was not unfamiliar to him. Somehow, my new attitude about sweets and other fattening foods grew more intense each day. Whenever I went shopping at the grocery market, I made damn sure several pints of Ben & Jerry's ice cream were in my cart. I also included chocolate chip cookies, Erik's favorite Gummy Bears, and caramel-filled candy.

In my hands a pint of ice cream wouldn't last me half an hour whenever I watched alone my favorite Saturday afternoon cartoons. Within two weeks my running weight jumped from 115 lbs to 130 lbs! My distances decreased even during the best of sunny days. A 15-mile run was child's play to me, compared to the 26-mile runs I had dared myself to complete. Before I knew it I couldn't properly fit into my dresses, skirts, pants, and running shorts because I was ballooning in the thighs, waist, hips, buttocks.

"Zae, if you don't turn things around," one of my female running buddies said to me one day over the telephone, "you gonna need to fetch a cane to help you get to the front door of your apartment."

"I'm trying; it'll happen, Tess."

"What you're doing to yourself is a crime. No man is worth killing yourself over. Look, it's not too late to think about a sensible diet plan – before it's too late."

Tess was a long distance runner I admired so much. Unlike me, she was tall and lanky and more strong willed. Even her cheer leading was no match for my post marriage rejection blues.

"Just stop eating ice cream for a while. French fries. Pasta. And teeth-roting candy. Try that routine for six months and you'll be back to normal."

I didn't get back to "normal". The less I felt enthused about weekend running, the more weight gain I packed onto my 5' 3" frame. I was unpleasantly chunky and sluggish. When early winter of that year arrived I weighed 180 lbs. I was looking like a whale about to breach on Oregon coastal waters. Nights of crying didn't solve my crisis. Lengthy telephone conversations – two thumbs up positive – failed to point the compass of my life back to normalcy. Layers of depression further crippled me, telling me that life wasn't worth living anymore, that no other man would grow in love with me anymore, that I should hate myself for being a loser and a quitter. In the deep recesses of my brain I could hear the faint echo of *kill yourself, Zae, kill yourself for your own good....*

Well, I didn't make any attempt to end it all during the early stages of my crisis. I just got bigger and bigger until I reached over 200 lbs. I hated the sad transformation reflected in my bedroom and bathroom mirrors but lacked the will power to save myself from total ruination. Most humiliating was how passing-by strangers (especially at my bus stops) would stare at me, some with pity, some with disdain, others with ridicule. I was no longer an attractive, sexy woman, I was an Alien Thing Blob capable of eating 100 lbs. of food daily. *Yuck!*

When my weight reached its peak of 260 lbs. and simple walking became a laborious physical crisis, I told myself to put an end to the madness. That date was Monday, September 10, 1990. My 29th birthday was less than six months away. I was going to reclaim the old Zae Rankin. A birthday gift to myself.

***

My search for full time employment was draining my energy and patience. I was unable to find the kind of employment that would allow me to speak and write French. My love for crafting poetry was stronger than ever but even that talent couldn't land me a job. I had a few thousand dollars in my savings account to tide me over for a certain period of time. I didn't want to go broke before then.

My lucky day happened when I boarded my regular evening schedule bus to return me to my Northeast Portland neighborhood predominately populated by African Americans. My neighbors to the right and left of my older apartment were the same kind of residents. By now, I was half the size of my blob-self and feeling awfully good about losing another 50 lbs. in the next four months. As long as I stuck to my campaign of no ice cream, candy, sugary sodas, pasta, and French fries.

A previous passenger had left behind a morning edition of the *Oregonian* Newspaper. Already, the employment ads faced me before I picked up the folded edition. Apparently, the passenger had circled in red ink employment ads of interest. I still wonder did that passenger gain employment after searching.

The marked ones were of no interest to me. I turned to the next page and read each one. The most interesting offer came from Camera World in downtown Portland. A customer service representative was needed... good pay, good hours, good benefits – a swaying carrot I couldn't resist.

Overnight I became more inspired and hopeful and decided to apply in person at Camera World. After a curious interview, discussion about my work history, (strong resume) and a brief tour of the business, the manager promised to give me an answer in a few days. When that time period ended, he indeed gave me a call back and asked if I could report for work the next Monday. And I did. No one else was happier than me that Monday. I saw the job as an opportunity to keep my mind off of Erik and how his mind set had altered my life.

What was going to happen next in my life took me by surprise. Was it going to be another episode of Roulette Fate, like my collaborator Raymond had discussed with me in the prologue?

A couple weeks into my new customer service job, graphic artist Matilda invited Tim Thornton and I on a hike to Larch Mountain, in the county of Multnomah, and its highest peak is 4,061 feet. (As an extinct volcano near Portland, the designated name of "larch" is misleading because no western larch can be found there. The North American species of coniferous tree, however, can be found in abundance in southwestern British Columbia, southwestern Alberta, eastern Washington, eastern Oregon, northern Idaho, and western Montana.) Tim was an Inside Salesman in the Mail Order Department; that was my additional title too.

Tall and athletically built, I was attracted to Tim from the start because he had a great sense of humor that had me laughing sometimes at inappropriate moments while on the job. Even over the telephone. A couple of times I had to give him a warning, fearing we both would be fired immediately. He had a head full of ginger brown hair that almost matched the color of his slightly hooded eyes. He took fastidious care of his complexion and was clean shaved. He liked wearing his favorite cologne: Brute.

That brisk autumn day of the hike on Larch Mountain Trail #441 showcased the wonders of nature in our Pacific Northwest paradise. Indigenous trees – pacific silver fir, grand fir, Douglas fir, and western hemlock – overwhelmed the senses with their ancient foliage – contrasting yellows, burnt reds, rich browns, and variegated orange leaves still attached to their root source, while expected non-survivors were ensconced on the ground... *crunch crunch crunch* underneath our feet. All an inviting canvas for outdoorsy artists to sketch or paint.

The raw aroma of not-for-human-consumption rotting fruit from trees and vines filling the air wasn't corrupted enough to make you want to cover your nose. Just another process to produce natural fertilization for the next growth of vegetation come spring 1990.

"When was the last time you hiked up here?" Tim asked me, as we stepped up to a higher level of walk path. He took the role as our leader.

I raised a hand; my other hand held a strapped water bottle.

"First time for me." I was used to running on flat surfaces. I didn't want to admit this form of hiking would sooner or later trigger my asthma. Not yet had I revealed to Tim and Matilda about my asthma condition. I had brought my rescue inhaler for a likely episode and it was stored in my backpack. I was still carrying around 30 extra lbs. of my own weight too. Did I dare tell Tim about my bittersweet history with Icelandic Erik? Would the truth reflect negatively on me? Make me more undesirable in his eyes? After all, he did seem interested in me and showed earlier signs of approval. In particular, I could tell he enjoyed taking sneaky looks at my full breasts and rounded, firm butt.

As an experienced rock climber whose arms and legs were beautifully crafted and made for rugged adventures, Matilda chuckled. Her voice was deeper than mine but not quite mannish. Her ash blond hair was tied in a ponytail, giving her angular face a slightly hawkish appearance. "Today marks my fifth ascent in two years. I never get bored doing it."

Tim stopped in his tracks and stretched his long arms outward. In admiration, he looked up at the surrounding forest canopy "Guys, how can you possibly get bored with nature, unless it's been attacked by toxic waste?"

Matilda and I chuckled.

"Thank goodness this one hasn't been harmed," Matilda said.

"Always something, huh?" I said, before we continued upward on the path.

Finally, after another mile and a half journey, we reached the summit of Larch Mountain. What a glorious 360 degree view of the majestic valley featuring snowcapped Mount Hood as a photographer's focal point. From my backpack, I removed my lunch, a fresh bottle of water, and a Kodak Instant 300 series camera. At the time, I didn't know that Sherrand Point Trail #443 provided an even more glorious view of Mount Adams, Mount Jefferson, Mount Rainier, and Mount Saint Helens.

Before I unfolded a thick peanut butter and jelly sandwich wrapped in aluminum foil, I asked Tim and Matilda to pose for me. They did a hilarious job of clowning in different poses until it was my turn to pose with Tim. We acted like jokers on a schoolyard but it was fun. They got along well as co-workers and seemed to trust each other after work hours. I sensed she was a matchmaker and perhaps wanted to see what kind of chemistry Tim and I would create. Already, we had an initial physical attraction chemistry just like I did with Eric. But was there a difference – a slight edge – in favor of Erik? I thought so. I still was willing to become better acquainted with Tim in other ways.

On reflection, gals and guys, how many single men does it take to court you until you find the most suitable one with the right fringe benefits? Is 10 too many? How about 25?

Our mountaintop discussions covered many topics, including hot button ones like abortion vs. pro-life issues; gun control vs. gun ownership rights; invasion of illegal aliens; higher taxation; and police brutality in poorer African American communities. None of those issues sparked division among us; each of us presented an open mind but without viable solutions.

It was almost 4:00 pm when we reached the floor of the valley. Before we reached Matilda's SUV, Tim was complaining about coolness of the air mingling with dripping sweat from underneath his mackintosh shirt. If unattended for a lengthy period, I told him, he could get sick. He dismissed my concern with an "oh well" shrug. But I was serious about the matter and decided to loan him my long-sleeved khaki shirt to reduce the chill. He thanked me for caring.

When Matilda parked her SUV into the parking lot of my Northeast Portland apartment, Tim handed me my shirt, and gave me a goodbye kiss on the cheek. I wanted to feel his manly hug and the possible sparks from it.

"Be a good little boy on your way home," I said, with a teasing smile.

Matilda winked at me, I winked back at her. "I'll keep a close eye on him, Zae. He's in good hands, so don't worry."

As crazy as it as this might sound, my hope for a better long term relationship with Tim Thornton Strusburger (shortening it to Tee Tee, at particular times of endearment) was so high in the clouds, that I took my khaki shirt to bed with me. I inhaled his musty, sweaty scent... not at all offensive to me... but a weird feeling of arousal tingled in my groin and made a path to my erect nipples. Somehow, I resisted the thrill of solo masturbation. The next morning, though, my bottom sheet was damp from overnight sweating.

After that first memorable hike, Tim invited me to dinner at one of his favorite Asian restaurants on NE Sandy Boulevard. The Zien Hong restaurant was a short walk from his two-bedroom apartment on Burnside Street. He told me he was an avid photography enthusiast and used the second bedroom as a temporary photo studio for his own pet projects. He was deeply knowledgeable about the subject and state of the art equipment used over several decades. I also had a strong interest in experimenting with photograph. I took candid shots of objects and people I deemed interesting. Eventually my work got noticed by other pro photographers, some of whom worked with nonprofit organizations back east, some who were acquainted with Tee Tee.

The more my heart felt safe with Tim, the more the memory of Icelandic Erik faded. During my fourth month of acquaintanceship with Tim, Erik sent me a two-page letter expressing his own kind of grief over his failure to commit himself to our then forthcoming marriage. I couldn't believe it when he confessed that he didn't inwardly feel strong enough to hold up to the pressures, the challenges, and the uncertain consequences of marital devotion. He was used to being a lover to multiple women whose health wasn't a factor. In other words, my bouts with asthma was a liability he preferred not to have to deal with. Also, he loved being an independent bachelor who could come and go and not be hung up by a possessive, jealous, and energy-draining wife. I wasn't going to respond in writing what I felt about his deceit but to myself I thought his confession was like several piles of seagull do-do. Why did he allow himself to stay attached to my life as long as he did, knowing already what he would ultimately do in the end? Surely, sex wasn't the glue that kept us together up until the Ultimate Moment. I gave of myself deep emotions expressing my love for him, showing psychological toughness to face hurtles, flexibility of mind, and a hunger to give birth to his children. That whole package wasn't good enough.

On one of our springtime walks late in the evening I shared my heartbreak over Erik with Tim. We held hands that night, like many other nights, as he patiently listened to a sad back story that should have been a dream come true. He surprised me when he didn't bad-mouth the Icelandic jilter; only offered nods and head shakes and emphasized how lucky he felt to be Erik's replacement. What woman wouldn't melt a little over hearing that compliment, then leaving behind a puddle that had accumulated around her feet?

I don't believe in magic because trained human manipulation brings it about, but I swear Tim "Tee Tee" Thornton seemed magical in the way he carried himself in public places. Both men and women were touched by his charisma, his charming smile, and his pitch fork self-confidence. He reminded me of the actor Fess Parker who portrayed the central character in the western frontier TV show *Davy Crockett*. In that role Mr. Parker was law-abiding, honest, fair, righteous, and upheld moral principles while facing wilderness dangers and dangerous villains. I truly believed that Tim would sacrifice his life to save mine, if such a predicament presented itself.

As the days, weeks, and months added up, we visited attractions Portland was most noted for its historical significance: The Grotto; Pittock Mansion; Diddler Beach; Memorial Coliseum; Delta Park; West Hills corridor of wealthy residents and their too expensive cars and homes. Our fondness for each other was like watching an infant grow stronger in stages. We didn't try to rush things in our new affair. We were laid-back during quiet moments and full of childlike wonder when it was playtime. Although I was spending more time "shacking up" (cohabitation these days) with Tim, we cooked meals at each other's apartment. I must admit he was better at cooking delicious creative meals. Sometimes, we would dress in the same style and colors when we went out to a special event. One time, we wore all white, including our shoes, which made us look like navy military personnel, or recently baptized church members on the march for Jesus.

What alerted me to the fact that Tee Tee was falling in love with me was during a Saturday night card game of Spades I taught him how to be a competitor.

After I won the first two rounds, he said to me, "I don't know how I could find a better match than the one I'm sitting across from." He raised his half-empty wine goblet and saluted me with it. "If we don't have too many fights about nothing, then we should get along just fine for years to come."

The spirit of his Santa Claus grin was all over my gaze and I thought song birds were singing from a distance, that church bells were ringing, and that my heart was beating faster against his excited heart.

"Well?" came his echo in my head.

I could barely reply. "Well... what?" I sipped wine to unclog my dry throat.

"Well, let's seriously think about sharing the rest of our lives together." He took my free hand; the fingers twitched as he kissed each finger. Why I didn't climax in my polka dot panties right then and there was another Zae Rankin mystery.

I told you earlier I don't believe in magic. We bought fresh premium oysters from renown supermarket chain Fred Myers. We liked to fry them. I was the one who found the making of a pearl that had segmented into three parts, almost resembling a rugged heart shape. Tim saved the creation and later had it crafted into a ring for me. He told me the jeweler said, "Your girlfriend won't like this ring because the pearl is imperfect." Tim replied with, "You don't know my girlfriend like I do. She's very sentimental. Romantic is her middle name."

The pearl ring was perfect enough for me and it will always remain a fond memory in my heart, even though some creep stole it (and a gold ring enhanced with two little horseshoes on it that my ex-fiancée Erik had given to me).

Not an engagement ring, see, though I boasted to fellow employees at PERS that it was. I felt that Tim was truly my soul mate; however, I've learned over the years that sometimes you lose one potential soul mate to gain another potential one. Meaning a broken heart can be mended over time, without extreme prejudice, and allowing a future marriage go-round to come into existence.

Although my relationship with Tim grew stronger in its own way day by day, we had long discussions about marriage, children of our own, sharing duties and responsibilities, dealing with unexpected difficulties, retirement, and the potential downfalls of divorce. We had decided that living together before marriage would be the proper way to test our faith in each other and to test the fabric strength of our compatibility. We figured less damage would occur if we decided to split in mid-stream and not have to deal with a divorce attorney, alimony, property division hassles, and lingering bitterness that could transition into hatred. We were well aware of the messy, highly contentious divorces of celebrities, wealthy professionals, and other notables. Sure, there would be hurt and sorrow if we did break up prematurely, but we would be spared dealing with all the other traumas.

Have you ever been *crazy* in love? That you can't get enough of being around, touching, squeezing, kissing, teasing, talking with your lover? Turning your hearts and minds into a kind of figurative mush? And getting heavy love sick blues when way too much inattentive time or long distance hurdles separate you two? Creating a temporary void?

Tim and I got entangled in that love net; got hooked from feeding each other the promises evoked by love, thereby forming for us a stronger bond of trust and faith. All good. However, we had our first big argument since the start of our relationship.

Sports vs. Comedy or Comedy vs. Sports. Those two TV activities had triggered that blow-out. I was a big fan of the Summer Olympics and watched them whenever free time permitted. Sometimes, I would tape the running competitions and watch later. As a former avid amateur runner who also enjoyed watching collegiate and pro running competitions, I wasn't a big fan of pro basketball under the authority of the NBA (National Basketball Association).

I can't give you any particular reason why that kind of sport hadn't appealed to; had nothing to do with how the game was dominated by African American males. I did recognize, however, the names of our local Portland Trailblazers heroes of 1991: Clyde Drexler, Terry Porter, Kevin Duckworth, and Jerome Kersey.

Unlike me, Tim was *fanatical* about the Trailblazers. He bought season tickets just for himself and usually attended Memorial Coliseum games with three of his best friends – each a fanatical fan. He bought their logo emblazoned uniforms, posters, duck-billed caps, bumper stickers, refrigerator magnets. In honor of Mr. Drexler, Tim named one of our beloved pugs "Clyde". Regardless, Tim bored me with his statistical knowledge of the star players and how he figured drafted college heroes would perform in the NBA.

Tim had a serious obligation to his mother that Round One playoff night (Sunday) and that's why he was unable to attend in-person the playoff competition; the Seattle Supersonics were the challengers. He asked me to tape that whole game so he could watch it later in the evening, around nine o'clock.

I had taken what I thought was a short nap but by the time I finally awakened, the game was in the half-time phase. I felt guilty for having overslept and incorrectly assumed that Tim wouldn't mind viewing the other half of the game. That didn't happen, either, because I decided to watch the wacky comedy show *In Living Color* featuring the Wayans clan: Marlon, Keenen, Ivory, Damon; and David Allan Grier, Jim Carey. In a later episode, Jennifer Lopez would make an appearance. The show produced some of the most clever gags and skits that usually cracked me up. The performers poked irreverent fingers at hot button issues dealing with race, sex, crime, prostitution, politics, and poverty.

Tee Tee couldn't corral his anticipation and excitement after he opened and slammed shut the living room door. The first words out of his mouth were, "*How many free throws did Drexler make each quarter? How many foul calls against him?*" He wasted no time cranking up the assumed taped whole game.

I yawned; I was ready for bed because I was facing another busy Monday workday at Camera World. "I didn't know I was supposed to be your statistics keeper. You didn't ask me."

He shot me a "I oughta slap your face off and stomp on it" glance as the tape reversed to the half-time segment. "Oh shit. Come on now". He jerked his head, clenched his jaws, then began staring at me, as if the sullen image he saw belonged to a complete stranger. "What the hell happened to the *first* half, Zae?" My lame explanation only made the situation less in my favor. "I told you what damn time the game was gonna start."

"I didn't fall asleep on purpose so you could miss any detail about the game."

"You can't do anything right!"

"That's not true and you know it!" The insult propelled me off the couch.

"I got fifty bucks bet on several categories... all on Drexler!" He made a gesture of tearing out his hair while his Portland Trailblazers duckbill cap still remained on his head.

"Not my problem." He stopped me from exiting.

"You're so dumb. Can't follow simple instructions. But an old dog can!"

"You know what?"

"Fucking dummy."

"Kiss my ass!"

"What a dumb fuck!"

Tim yanked off his beloved cap and threw it at me. Like a savage beast just escaped from a steel cage, he raced about the living room looking for an ink pen or pencil to write on blank paper. If only for this instance, he showed me that he cared more about recording statistics than he cared about massaging the ruffled feathers of my emotions. He created some doubts that hadn't existed before during the early stages of our romance. I saw them as a future complication.

As I headed for bed – knowing full well that he would attempt to have oral sex after a cool down period in the wee hours – I heard him call me a bunch of dumb bitches, interspersed with, "Come on... you Seattle idiots... keep fouling Drexler. Four more and I'll win half my fuckin' bet!"

Tim and I cohabited for a lengthy time before we married. He was 38. I was 29. From renters we became homeowners. We lived in a small two-bedroom rental house at the time of our wedding, and we had immensely enjoyed living there since 1990. It was near Mt. Tabor Park (another ancient Pacific Northwest volcano). And the neighboring trees were blooming, their pink flower petals dancing to the ground like a ballet, gracefully. We enjoyed walking adventures in our Mt. Tabor Neighborhood, where we often visited our favorite restaurant Zien Hong. Their service was quick – food fresh and hot. Our other adventures included lengthy hikes, visits to art galleries, museums, movie houses. We also explored other historical Portland neighborhoods.

The mowed lawn of our backyard competed for attention with a mini-jungle of Elephant grass, flowery weeds, and an assortment of fruit growth: plums, blackberries, raspberries. Neighbors' curious cats usually roamed our paradise. One colorful Norwegian-born neighbor we nicknamed "Mr. Mumbles" because he always mumbled when he wasn't wearing his dentures. His actual name was Aksel Bakken. His Tabby cat Polly, one of the roamers in our backyard, had fleas. Instead of using the *appropriate* remedy, his creativity went way beyond the norm. I witnessed him vacuum cleaning Polly! She complained with meows, but was otherwise obedient.

Another disturbing time I witnessed Polly staggering in our backyard. Looked very strange and I wondered if somehow she hurt herself. When she started staggering in a circle and meowing oddly, I knew something was wrong. Her eyes were glassier and too shifty. I stared at her body, hoping a knife–tip or other sharp-tipped object hadn't pierced it. The absence of feline blood anywhere gave me a degree of relief.

I called out her name several times as she seemed to navigate toward an unintended pathway leading back to Mr. Mumbles property and concrete driveway. Curious, I trailed her steps.

The door of his two-car garage was opened. When I called out his name, poor Polly collapsed, rolled to her right side, went into a violent tremble, and then stiffened. Her meowing stopped abruptly.

"Please. No, god. Don't let her die," I said to myself, approaching the garage. Tim and I didn't dare call him by our designated nickname. "Mr. Bakken?" No response. He did have a percentage of hearing loss. "Can you hear me?!" About a minute crawled by and still no response. I knelt beside Polly and discovered she was still breathing. "MR. BAKKEN! SOMETHING'S WRONG WITH POLLY!"

I felt relieved when I heard his feet shuffle down the half dozen steps of his deck. Then I saw his slight, emaciated-looking frame topped off by a puffball of wiry white hair.

"We-l-ll. Hel-lo Zae." Bifocal eyeglasses magnified his puzzlement. He glanced from me to Polly. "What is your urgency?"

I explained to him how she was staggering in our backyard.

"She not feeling like cat past three days," he replied, his glum face nodding. "A cold or something."

"Maybe you should take her to your vet, if you have one, sir."

"*Ja, selvfølgelig.* Me wait." He raised fingers. "My Polly lick two teaspoons of medicine."

"Okay." I was skeptical.

Toothless Mr. Mumbles grinned and the reaction restored temporary pinkness to his face. He seemed proud of his pet parental deed.

But what kind of feline medicine? I thought, then asked, "Why did it make her act strangely?"

He hunched his bony shoulders. "I give her what I take for winter colds...Robitussin."

My stunned expression told him I didn't believe what I heard.

"Jesus... *Robitussin?* I felt blood drain from my face. "When?"

"Thirty minutes ago."

"No, Mr. Bakken. Only for *human* consumption. That's why she was staggering like a drunk adult. Go now... to your vet – *hurry!*"

"*Ja, selvfølgelig.*" Ashamed, he covered his thin lips, shook his head, and his eyes started misting.

I knew what those Norwegian words meant in English, "yes, of course", but I had to ask for translation after he concluded with: "*Jeg vil fa henne til å føle seg bedre før vi drar på ferie.*" ("I want to make her feel better before we go on holiday.")

During the evening hours of that day I still felt empathy for poor Polly – had not been rushed to any vet – whose intoxicated-like condition was downgraded to an approaching normalcy. Because I was used to consuming legal drugs for my asthma condition and other ailments, the pharmaceutical names would sound like science fiction. Unbeknownst to me, I discovered that the trade name Robitussin contains two active ingredients: dextromethorphan (can increase the risk of drowsiness in older people) and guaifensin (an expectorant that helps loosen up and thins phlegm); inactive ingredients include propylene glycol, sucralose, fructose corn syrup.

Robitussin overdose in humans can cause a number of physical side effects in addition to mental changes: slurred speech, poor coordination, sweating, nystagmus (a rapid, uncontrollable jittery movement of the eyeballs), dry mouth, constipation, muscle spasms, muscle stiffness, heart arrhythmias. Furthermore, the CIA experimented with dextromethorphan during the late 1940s and late 1950s. The agency had to come up with a chemical formula similar to codeine to help reduce soldiers fear of dying on the battlefield. Stress and psychological factors were reduced after dextromethorphan was administered.

The chances are good that Polly and her master Mr. Bakken aren't alive today. He took to his grave his typical twisted thinking for solving pet circumstances. Maybe she produced sets of kittens to represent her genes, without the side effects of Robitussin....

Our wedding day was May 14, 1991. I remember feeling nervous but the one thing that was paramount was that Tim's relatives, who had been staying with us the past week, would be going to a motel that night after our reception. Hearing that decision was significant because Tim's German-born father Hans and mother Sigfried, (she in particular) was an annoying busybody all week telling me how to do the housework. She was an East Berliner during the November 9, 1989 destruction of the infamous Berlin Wall (symbol of power and control of a Soviet-led communist bloc facing collapse). I had been biting my tongue on several occasions so as to not say anything that would piss her off. This happened on the previous day, repeatedly saying to me, "You need to wipe the sides of the toilet; can't you see the condensation there?"

I tried to explain to her that it didn't matter how many times you wiped the sides of the toilet, the condensation would return every five minutes. But to no avail, she still kept harping on the subject.

"You need plumber... fix right away." She was staring at the older toilet.

"Maybe not." I let out a sigh of frustration. "It's not hurting me."

Her puffy face turned redder as she wagged a finger. "You call him tomorrow. Water... it will spill everywhere."

It was all I could do to prevent myself from screaming, "WHY DON'T YOU DO IT YOURSELF! THEN GO BACK TO GERMANY TONIGHT!"

Morning hours before the afternoon wedding....

I was still in my short red robe after a shower when Tim took a photo of me, the first of our wedding day. My cheeks were red with inflammation due to the sinus infection and my short brown hair was brushed away from my face. In the photo, I had a furrowed brow – a look of pain on my face, even though I was smiling. My father-in-law Hans, a gentle soul whose English needed help, showed more empathy for my situation than my self-righteous, snobbish mother-in-law. We exchanged few words after we finished breakfast.

My wedding dress was eggshell white, gathered down the bodice with boning on the sides and long lace sleeves. It was "physical evidence" left behind from when I was supposed to marry my first fiancée Icelandic Erik. As you know, he abandoned me, our dreams, our future.

Our wedding was simple and inexpensive because it was held at our rental house and officiated by a judge. In attendance were Tim's parents, my mom and step dad, my maternal grandparents, my best friend Kendall and her boyfriend Don, and Tim's friend Hwan. Tim and I had each written our own wedding vows.

The ceremony went smoothly, with the exception of Tim's mother Sigfried who didn't shield her cynical expression because of our wedding footwear: Tim's spit-shined tan cowboy boots and my red cowboy boots. She held a camera but not once did she take a photo of us while wearing the boots. I felt certain she didn't like me as a person and – from her foreigner point of view – for being the underclass American who claimed her son from her. I didn't like her overall attitude but I wanted to keep the peace and protect my budding marriage.

We quietly celebrated with champagne before a total of eleven of us ventured to the Zien Hong Restaurant, where we huddled at a revolving round table and demolished a seven-course meal. Later that night, Tim and I watched the movie *The Princess Bride* then made love afterwards. In the wee hours, I dreamed of Hans Strusburger divorcing his wife.

The next morning, I awakened with intense pain in my sinuses behind my cheeks – the maxillary sinus cavities. Which meant I had another sinus infection and it was taxing my patience; I had suffered from such infections since I was 17.

On that same day, my doctor had given me some pain medication along with an antibiotic. I took my medications. Eventually, the customary pain subsided.

* * *

Oceanside, Oregon… the less populated location of our fall honeymoon period. Most days were cloudy and stormy but for us it was a calming, happy time. All that clean and crisp ocean air… caressing our smiling faces… therapeutic for our minds and souls. We thought we'd remain in love Forever and a Day and disallow any circumstance to divide us. Wishful thinking at its best, I suppose.

We nestled in a shingled rustic bungalow overlooking the Pacific Ocean. Our eyes feasted on two memorable seascape sunsets as we drank French wine. Several times, we had to chase away hungry raccoons from our quarters – even after we had tossed them cheddar cheese chunks. Not until later did we become fully aware that raccoons carry roundworm bacteria (*Baylissascaris procyonis*) that's lodged in their feces and can be harmful to humans.

We ended our Oceanside honeymoon more united, greedily in love, and hoping for a bright and productive future together. The mighty fuses that helped keep the intricacies of our marriage perking, however, would be shattered.

CHAPTER EIGHT

HIT AND RUN CRIME UNSOLVED

Why do many tragedies happen around the weeks leading to Christmas? Why mysterious house fires that take the lives of entire families, destroy thriving businesses, and nature's forests? Or a beloved community member who has a history of generosity is robbed and killed and the perpetrator is never caught and punished? And how about the newborn infant whose future seems promising and bright but dies in her crib, thereby traumatizing her young parents (guilt-ridden) whose marriage ends in a bitter divorce? Are these fate-bound examples destined to happen?

A reliable new friend in the future would characterize such outcomes as "ROULETTE FATE". Certainly not Las Vegas-style gaming machinery odds, he would explain to me when we would share one of his go-to dinner recipes. He equated it with circumstances out of our control, whether or not the "victim" is innocent, honorable, popular, god-fearing, or having the psychotic disposition of cannibal serial killer Jeffrey Dahmer.

A few days before Christmas, I got off work from PERS (State of Oregon Public Employes Retirement System; the former location was at SW Market and SW 3rd Avenue in downtown Portland) and I went shopping for Christmas gifts for my husband Tim. I wanted to see him looking jazzy in fancy shirts, one with an abstract design in black, gray, and cream colors, another in greenish brown. Gift selections, also, for my parents, stepparents, sister and brother.

My solo time spent shopping for gifts was fun and inspiring, even though fellow shoppers were in their competitive modes to take full advantage of out-of-this-world deals and bargains.

With my shopping mission gratefully completed several hours later, I hustled three full shopping bags to my regular bus stop. Every step in the two-block journey my face was throbbing with pain due to chronic sinusitis and infection in my sinus cavities located in my cheeks (maxillary sinuses). Similar infections had been a crisis for me since I was 17, and continued onward even though I had one sinus surgery at St. Vincent Hospital six months prior to this day. (The surgeon made openings called "windows" in my maxillary sinuses, but I still continued to have recurrences.)

This day was more than about gift shopping; it gave me a sense of hope, of conquering my future addictions and other medical demons. Was it possible I *could* reinvent myself?

I was ready to board my scheduled bus. I approached the busy intersection of SW Madison and Fifth Avenue. I had to cross to the other side of the crosswalk to the bus stop. The weather was cool and approaching dusk. With three stuffed shopping bags I stood on the corner, waiting for the pedestrian signal to flash *WALK!*

Other foot traffic was dwindling.

A minute later, I stepped into the walkway cross walk. At that moment, I saw a driver (was hard for me to identify which gender) in a dark colored SUV concerned about dashing to make a right corner turn but, without using common sense, made an illegal dash to the left lane. I thought I was a target because the front side of the SUV smacked the hell out of the right side of my body, the side which I was holding two shopping bags. The willful hit sent me flying into approaching traffic, but few people witnessed the incident. My pain was worse than a bulldozer running over me. I was gasping for air as I crawled to safety. My alarmed adrenaline fought against the shock of the situation. No human came to my aid. There was pounding in my head. I started aching all over. The careless driver wasn't a Good Samaritan; he or she just sped away, unconcerned about any degree of possible injury to me. I never saw the SUV's license plate number.

My Christmas gift purchases littered the crosswalk. I scrambled to retrieve each one and secure them in the damaged shopping bags. I managed to succeed before traffic would turn into a real bitch.

I was too fearful to report this matter to the police department and have the mystery driver face a circuit court judge on a criminal charge of malicious hit-and-run. Because the driver's identity still remains a mystery, I could not file a claim against his/hers insurance policy.

A week later, I decided I should see my doctor for an examination. I was fully bruised on my right side; I suppose I was lucky in not suffering more serious trauma like death. The diagnosis: I had the medical condition named fibromyalgia, meaning the nerve centers of my body were acutely damaged. Future pain management would require heavy doses of painkillers. Even today, I consume various sedatives, morphine, and methadone to help control the pain. At times, it can become a torturer. My body's left side looked like a black and blue abstract painting with grayish highlights.

The doctor was so concerned that he said to me, "If your husband assaulted you, it's also my duty to report him to the police."

His accusation stunned me. The words rushed out, *"Oh no. Tim's not responsible. An unidentified driver in an SUV hit me and took off."* He looked even more skeptical and suspicious. Didn't matter to me.

Two days later, my pain from the hit and run had turned severe all over my body, making concentrating on anything more difficult. For two years I was *undiagnosed* with anything other than chronic pain for which my primary doctor gave me Tylenol 3 (acetaminophen and codeine) and Soma, a powerful muscle relaxant.

In the beginning, before I was diagnosed with Fibromyalgia by five rheumatologists, my car insurance company gave me $500 for the "accident" and persuaded me to sign a waiver that would bar me from seeking a larger settlement. Maybe that was because no other citizens came forth as witnesses to the crime (only the bone-headed driver was a witness), so I naively accepted the $500 offer. A credibility issue overshadowing the stingy payoff? Perhaps my insurance company thought the whole matter was a scam.

Two years later, I was changed (not my choice) to a different health plan through PERS and had to change primary care doctors who sent me to those five rheumatologists who all agreed I had Fibromyalia caused by the accident. They also diagnosed me with Lupus; it was unrelated to the hit and run. Lupus is an autoimmune disorder in which the various organs and tissues become inflamed by an overactive immune response, an attack of those tissues and organs as if they were foreign.

Eventually, the rheumatologists took me off the pain medication and the Soma and put me on amitriptline; the antidepressant was supposed to relieve nerve pain but didn't for me. Flexeril was another muscle relaxant. I also consumed Ibuprofen and Plaquenil for the Lupus. My pain was complex, thus it required the appropriate medications. Plaquenil seemed to help the Lupus symptoms (sores on scalp, positive ANA (antinuclear antibodies); Raynaud's disease – smaller arteries that provide less circulation in fingers and toes due to cold weather or stress, then joint pain, and Interstitial Cystitis – inflammation of the bladder.

I became allergic to the Ibuprofen, requiring me to try other anti-inflammatories but they also triggered allergic reactions in me.

My fibromyalgia was relentless, growing more chronic. Desperate for an uncomplicated, simple solution, I thought drinking wine would help me… serve as self-medication. At first, that new approach entailed drinking small amounts of low potency wine. My will power suffered at the task. Soon I was binging…drinking much more wine until I became addicted. No denying it, the hit and run crime was more responsible for my pivotal downfall – physically, mentally, emotionally, spiritually.

I would be thrust into a rabbit hole, where temptations of depravity would be fulfilled, where escape from more sickness was impossible, where a failed suicide attempt didn't teach me a lesson, where job losses mounted, and where the broken bones of a failed marriage lay.

As was mentioned in the prologue, abuser Johnny Rahwaye, an apartment renter, "evicted" me for being sneaky about drinking alcohol. He had given me only two hours to gather all of my belongings. While he was talking on the phone in the living room, I was busy stuffing clothes into two suitcases. At times, I would take small breaks so I could sip from a plastic cup containing vodka and orange juice. What the hell. The bastard was going to kick me out anyway.

With burglar-like caution I opened the bedroom door and peeked down the hallway. The smell of marijuana drifted toward me. I made a final decision because I never wanted to see his disgusting face again. Especially after he had raped me and socked me in the jaw.

His old duplex apartment was built with a kitchen door, from which led to a neglected backyard and a dilapidated wood fence. Three slats were missing, proving a gap wide enough to accommodate my escape to the next-door-neighbor's driveway, and beyond. My car was waiting. I didn't want to use it again as a sleeping shelter.

My suitcases in hand, I escaped from the frying skillet to a fire storm. Regardless, I was determined to arrive safely at the apartment of my friend Myrtle. I could get high there. She was responsible for introducing me to crack cocaine and becoming my "pimp madam".

Less than a week later, Myrtle was at her promoting best. She reintroduced me to a familiar man named Chris who, when high on crack cocaine, hungered for oral sex. Lucky for us, my jaw no longer felt fractured.

Myrtle was a genuine cutthroat personality. She possessed a deep, arrogant voice that projected an argumentative spirit. She stood a thick-shouldered 5' 9", somewhat stocky and muscular. She looked like she could pulverize you from head to toe in a street corner fight.

That smoke crack session night Myrtle said to Chris, "You can have a piece of my top bitch if you give me a fiddy." In other words, $50 could buy enough crack to keep an average abuser high for half an hour. She already had turned me into a crack whore.

"You got yourself a deal." Chris, a retired long distance trucker as thin as a broomstick, licked his lips as he guided me to Myrtle's 'ho busting' bedroom that vaguely resembled the cheapness of a roadside motel room.

Impatient to re-experience the heavenly euphoric rush and peace of such a high, we smoked a few crack nuggets before we undressed. From past experience I discovered that some men high on crack are prevented from penile erection, in contrast to their mentally stimulated desires for sex. Poor Chris was a victim.

I had a reputation for getting the "job" done... making a man ejaculate within a specific time. Not Chris. He was pushing past 50 years old. At the half hour mark, he still was as flaccid as a wet dollar bill. Honestly, I cared less about his desire for conclusive satisfaction. I was riding on a cloud of immense pleasure and feathery lightness and I wanted to attain what could extend to an even *higher* level.

Between breaks we smoked more crack (all along increasing my addiction) for another half hour. I returned to the "job". He ended being one of the few crack-addicted men I could not get off.

Cutthroat Myrtle got her own high satisfaction. After she got an advance crack baggie deal from a sexually discontented Chris and watched him exit her apartment, she coldly emphasized to me in the living room,"*Did you make that motherfucker come?*"

"He resisted." My crack high was fading; my body needed another fix, and soon. I hugged myself against a sudden coldness between us. I knew Myrtle wasn't going to share with me her advanced, pay-you-later baggie. "Not my damn fault." She stiffened. Her blood-shot eyes stared through me. She stepped closer, towered over me, and telegraphed her intention to spring into violence.

"He's one of my best tricks, bitch. He always keep crack handy!"

"Next time, you do him." Saying that got me an immediate slap to the side of my face where Johnny Rahwaye had slugged me. I didn't cry; the remnants of my high lessened the sting.

"Look at you... can't suck a cock right anymore!"

I flinched when Myrtle faked like she was going to ram her fist down my throat. "Next time, I'll do a better job. Give me a break." I attempted to rise but she pushed me back down on the hide-a-bed sofa. In the past, I had slept on it numerous times. Drunk to the hilt, a sorry-ass creature who no longer cared about self-dignity... just the next bottle of vodka and crack-filled pipe.

"I want you out of here by tomorrow morning," Cutthroat Myrtle warned.

"What?" The announcement snatched my breath away. "Are you *serious?*" She didn't need to be cruel. A man not ejaculating couldn't be that important.

"Stop by to visit another time," she said, then wagged the crack baggie in front of my face.

I attempted but failed to snatch it from her fingers.

She laughed like it was the world's best punchline. She had the upper hand over my addiction and she was aware I was willing to do *anything* for a tidbit worth of crack.

"After you wash your nasty ass, get in bed. Naked. We got us some talkin' to do, bitch. And you better follow my instructions."

Never before had I felt so alone, useless, homeless. Because of my addictions, I had burnt many bridges of friendship. I couldn't bug my parents about welcoming me back home. My brother was equally apprehensive about having me stay with him. (He did allow me to stay a few days only because he feared my alcohol drinking could get him evicted.) My ex-boyfriends hated me. I had enough money to pay for a three-day hotel room rental. After that, I would be broke.

My feeling highly vulnerable was akin to a naked little girl on stage and gawked at by an auditorium of naked old men. Tomorrow morning was a handful of hours away. I needed to make a decision before dawn. Sweet-talking Cutthroat Myrtle to allow me at least a week to get myself together was out of the question, unless I could give her more crack than she could smoke in an hour. After all, she was more of a hardcore smoker than me.

Believe it or not, I decided to return to Johnny Rahwaye's apartment. He was flippant about my request when I showed up at his doorstep the following evening, with my two packed suitcases and a worn-out fragile body and mind.

He was the stuff of nightmares… the ugliest man I knew – both inside and out. He didn't look quite so unappetizing the last time I saw him. Now his skin was a ghostly white, the pallor of death. His eyes held the look of a hardened criminal. His cheeks were sunken and his greasy, unwashed hair was thinning. Was his nose flattened by the head-on collision with a truck? When I had first met him, (after my recent eviction due to rent nonpayment) he was reluctant to tell me about a particular injury. His left thigh had a chunk of flesh ripped off then sewn back by a surgeon. The disfigurement happened when he caused his car to crash and flip over. He was ejected. Somehow, that leg got trapped under the chassis.

He was high on heroin.

Before I got myself entangled with Johnny, I got assistance from my former next-door-neighbor Doug. He didn't want to see me and my Scottie dog Jona living in my car. He was kind enough to offer me temporary shelter. Eventually I slept with him a couple of times when I was drunk. Perhaps he thought sex with him was going to be ongoing.

Living with him was working out okay but his apartment was located in a working class N.E. Portland neighborhood that had seen better days before re-gentrification (whites and others fleeing before blacks returned) and the crack epidemic. Bold roaches crawled over floors and walls, dominating the small, cluttered space. I recommended he use an eradication paste. Instead, he bought boric acid (making sure Jona wasn't in reach of it). His solution failed.

I would qualify for clean-and-sober housing after my short stint with Doug. No pet companions allowed there – that's why he agreed to take care of Jona at his place. I was able to visit with her everyday and take her for walks. I was attending AA and NA meetings until I weakened to temptation and bought a bottle of cooking wine with my food stamps. As you would expect, the violation ended my housing. Doug reluctantly agreed to take me back in, probably more for Jona's sake than my own.

Eventually he would kick me out because his girlfriend was jealous of me staying with him. He must have pitied me when he took me to stay with, of all people, his friend Johnny Rahwaye!

During this period I was a total wreck of a human being. I drank a lot of booze everyday until I puked my guts out. The task of "drying" out was difficult and painful. Pacing every night. Sweating profusely. Dry heaves. And the withdrawals were even more torturous. Waves of heat would wash over my body, then later chills would ravish it. Worst, a great burning in my stomach was attributed to inflammation of my pancreas. Sitting or lying down further aggravated the condition. My assumed alcohol placebo for the fibromyalgia was a dud.

I didn't, shamefully, give Jona the love, respect, and attention she deserved. In her own way she was a trooper with a stronger will to live and to be happy. We had endured the slings and arrows of life, not knowing if we'd have a certain future. You don't put a loved one like her in perilous circumstances. My addiction to booze and crack could have ended my life much sooner if she weren't a major part of my hazy, useless life.

God... I was too blinded to reach out to Him and have His redeeming grace bestowed upon me. As a little girl, I was more religious focused. Those out-of-school vacations on my grandparents Double Horseshoe Farm in Vale included Sunday service attendance at one of its few churches. I loved Sunday school, reading bible scriptures, helping raise funds for various church causes focused on the needs of elderly churchgoers, food pantry drives, and building expansion drives.

I suppose he wasn't done with me yet, for in ways he was keeping me alive for a higher purpose I could not comprehend. Still, that purpose was like a faraway mirage of palm trees, caressed by a warm breeze, and I imagined myself ready to quench my thirst for irresistible ice cold drinks arranged on a picnic blanket. Yet I would continue to be another despicable female human being crawling toward salvation, forgiveness, self-healing, and self-love.

Back in the bucket of no shame. Johnny apologized to me for having acted like an asshole the night he forced me to do a fake sex act on his long barrel .38 Smith & Wesson. He swore it was done to scare me back to my senses, to help me stop abusing crack and vodka, to dissuade me from being sneaky about hiding vodka bottles, and to prevent my temptation to steal money from him. He himself had 14 years of sobriety from heroin, yet he later confessed that he had visited a next-door neighbor and shot up with him. He pointed out that two addicts living together wasn't a great scenario.

You don't give a known, previously convicted pyromaniac a box of wooden matches and hope like hell she doesn't set your Beverly Hills palatial mansion ablaze. In my case, Johnny thought his offering – of all screwy things… a *bottle of wine* would bury the hatchet between us and all would be forgiven. Did he really want to see me dead? He was well aware that even the low alcohol content of wine was enough to trigger my vodka binging!

And that's exactly what happened four days later.

His "peace pipe" offering was only a ploy to get me high enough to trick me into having sex with him, knowing full well that was the only way I would be tempted to indulge.

He had tricked me several times before and afterward I hated him and hated myself more. That last time, I could barely strip down naked and clean myself in the bathtub, before he banged his way into the bathroom, as drunk as a dozen skunks, gripping his erection, and demanding I wrap my lips around it. His total lack of respect for me and his nasty attitude left an indelible impression on my soggy brain, but I had promised myself that if he pulled the ploy again, I would drop a dime on him and have the police arrest him for sexual harassment.

This time, though, I was minutes away from drowning in the same bathtub that Saturday night. I had reached a higher level of depression, hopelessness, depravity. I was going broke, I was jobless, I was homeless, my ex-husband despised me, and I was too spacey to embrace the love and affection of my current unofficial service animal.

Like a stone cold deranged woman, I had earlier purchased four gallons of cheap, fortified peach wine. Certainly no match for my beloved vodka, but I didn't care and the whole world didn't mean a fucking thing to me. By ten in the morning, I had emptied the first gallon. Johnny Rahwaye, thankfully, wasn't around to bug me about sex. I didn't know what time he would return.

After I got naked, I turned on a portable TV and switched to a channel featuring reruns of classic cartoon characters from the late 60s: *The Flintstones, The Jetsons, Mr. Magoo, Donald Duck, Porky Pig, Daffy Duck, Bugs Bunny.* I loved the last three characters because, whenever they had conflict with dastardly characters who wanted to commit great physical violence against them (and it happened), they'd spring right back to life and pursue justice for themselves. Sometimes these characters would flatten like ironed clothing multiple times but their stuff of *resilience* always amazed me! Sure, I knew it was just a planned plot of animation designed to pacify little kids so they could laugh their heads off in the positive spirit of fun.

At the time, I didn't see the connection between my notched predicaments and their cartoon predicaments. Nonetheless, resilience was deeply ingrained in my own historical genes. Of which I still didn't appreciate until I would embrace the "gospel" of self-rehabilitation, self-dignity, and self-love. Getting to each of those summits would require of me to go far beyond the strength and fortitude I had shown when I was a top-fit, competitive university student row crewmember.

Now that the first gallon of peach wine was history, my alcohol buzz acted like a slow teaser. I flashed back to vodka's potency and how it made me feel when I lowered to my knees and slid the second gallon from beneath the bed. The bottle was still chilled against my fingers as I guzzled the equivalent of a cup worth. I wanted to smoke cigarettes in the backyard but I feared Johnny Rahwaye would return home sooner than later and catch me off guard. What would he do if he caught me with my last three gallons?

Another cartoon began airing and each ridiculous scene made me laugh so hard that I started farting musically. My head felt like an inflated balloon because I was climbing higher to where I wanted to be. If this was my last day alive on planet Earth, then at least I would be rid of all of the nasty, sewer-like baggage my life had accumulated since my initial downfall among downfalls. As far as I was concerned, I was finished being a real human being.

After I peed in the bathroom for what seemed like half an hour, I staggered to the hide-de-hole where the fourth gallon awaited my consumption. But before I could unscrew the gallon's top, I passed out. The urge to pee again woke me an hour later, around 6 pm.

I was as sweaty as a chain gang prisoner on a cotton plantation, so I turned on the hot water knob, balanced myself on the toilet, and stared at the meandering steam. All I wanted to do was soak for about half an hour, then resume drinking more wine. Somehow, I had enough common sense left to make me realize I needed to cool down the half-filled tub of steaming water.

The last thing I remembered after I eased into the tub was the significance of white gown sinners being re-baptized in river water and how a new awakening would give the cleansed sinners new hope for a new direction toward redemption. What happened next should have been for me the Ultimate Wakeup Call. Here again, a hard head makes a sore butt.

Believe it or not, Johnny Rahwaye *saved* my miserable life! He told me shocking details that made me think that God's grace was what kept me alive; that He wasn't done with me yet; that He kept me alive for a purpose I did not yet realize.

Johnny and I had occupied the living room. We were sharing a joint.

"If I had stayed at the race track for one more race, bitch," Johnny said, "you'd be dead meat on a medical examiner's table."

Apparently, Johnny was broke and unable to place a bet on the sixth race at Portland Meadows Race Track, so he left and drove back home. He went to the kitchen. He made a sandwich. He entered the living room. He turned on the TV. Several minutes later was when he heard water running in the main bathroom. The time was 10:25 pm. Another ten minutes went by.

"I still can't believe how you figured something wasn't right," I said to him, feeling like I didn't deserve to continue living. The shock from the ordeal seemed to haunt me.

"Shit. Didn't sound like you was taking a motherfucking shower." Johnny inhaled the weed smoke deeper into his lungs, causing tears to spring from his eyes as he choked "Another thing: when I headed back to the kitchen I saw puddles of water flowing from the bottom of the goddamn bathroom door."

I shook my head; I still couldn't recall that detail. He further explained that he called out my name, twice, before he twisted the doorknob. I didn't remember locking the door.

"I took my fist and pounded that sumbitch but you didn't make a fucking sound. Scared the shit outta me." Recounting the awful experience made him wipe sweat off his forehead. "I had a decision to make, okay. Decided to ram my foot until the door flung open."

That detail, too, made me shiver; it also renewed my guilt and shame.

"Why didn't you call 911?" I said.

"Help otherwise, asshole, would've been too late."

"I can't thank you enough for saving my life." I wrapped a pink baby blanket tighter around me. Never before had I felt deeply in a trench of loneliness, of uselessness, of doom. I was reluctant to pray to God, hoping His power would deny Johnny Rahwaye the temptation of using me as a greater sex slave because of how he saved my life. One thing was certain: Johnny would never change his nasty, diabolical ways.

"I know a little something about CPR. That's what I did on you for almost twenty minutes. I'm glad as hell you came back; I was *begging* you to do so."

Johnny also told me I had coughed and shook and gasped for air… much like a fish popped out of beach water and flopping around on hot sand.

"I didn't want no police coming here to investigate your death. I was holding the good shit for one of my Tacoma partners."

I forced a grin. "Better quality crack?"

"Hell naw… crystal meth."

I had already heard about horror stories associated with that crazy stuff and how it made meth addicts in general even more dangerous and unpredictable. Crack and alcohol were my limits of addiction. Smoking weed was no big deal to me but it did boost my appetite.

I didn't want to pray to God in front of Johnny. He probably would have clowned me for days before kicking me out again. If only he knew how my present life felt like: a bowl of gelatin, resilient when lightly poked, breaking under more intense pressure.

Losing self-dignity is a devastating insult to your own humanity. Not caring about your mental and physical health, your safety, your loved ones, and the future you is another blow to your weakening ego. If it weren't for Johnny Rahwaye's voyeuristic lustfulness whenever I got stoned and passed out into oblivion, I would have not been a victim of gang rape by so-called friends whom I thought were my protectors. I will spare you much of the ugly circumstances and later tell you more about my former boyfriend Damon.

You have already been introduced to cut-throat Myrtle who became my "pimp madame" and stingy crack supplier. For an undisclosed amount of crack for herself, she set me up to be sexually abused by three of her male friends and Johnny Rahwaye. Her spare bedroom was the scene of the crimes. Way too much vodka and crack had put me under, deeply. Preventing me from discovering the truth, of which Damon, somehow, found out first. The four culprits had repeatedly raped me. Afterward, I had terrible hot flashes, fever-like symptoms, dizziness, and nausea so bad I couldn't even think about eating food.

Because those conditions persisted for almost a week, I decided to make an appointment with my gynecologist. Test results both stunned and horrified me. One or more of the rapists had transmitted the venereal disease chlamydia into my vagina.

Much later, I found out through another source that one of the rapist's girlfriend had the same disease. I was given the appropriate medication, hoping I would heal without serious complications.

I forced myself to cut off all ties to Myrtle and her creepy friends, Johnny Rahwaye, and my abuse of alcohol and crack. But I didn't expect to be haunted by nightmares depicting vaginal/anal rape, torture, and dismemberment.

In spite of more personal trauma headed in my direction, the core of my being would prepare me for more downfalls caused by my actions, my husband Tim, and other forces out of my control.

Those who fail to see the historical significance of when the roaming rabbit aims the hunting rifle are doomed to be its human prey... again. (My paraphrase from an *abaca* fiber refrigerator magnet designed by a Portland visual artist.)

CHAPTER NINE

AFTERMATH AND THE PAINS FROM HELL

Despite our mostly happy marriage, Tim and I decided to get a divorce because of my addiction to alcohol. I have often wondered if that hit and run crime hadn't occurred would our marriage survived until only death screwed us apart. Took three months for the divorce decree to become reality. We settled out of court. I received my share of the mortgage paid which was about $22,000.

When we first separated, Tim refused to give me any time to collect my property and to find another place to live. But my mom intervened and convinced him to give me at least two weeks of move-out time. She traveled from Philomath to Portland to help me pack. My friend Kendall accompanied me in my rental search. We found a green, older two-bedroom house with a monthly $675 payment.

Bonnie and I moved in. The transition was tough for us because we missed the other members of our little family: Tim, Clyde, and Sisely. Bonnie, in particular, was more depressed. That's why I decided to get her an animal companion… mixed breed canine Harry came in to our lives.

My rental house was located near Mt. Tabor Park. I would either run in the neighborhood (six miles) or walk him up to the park and let him off the leash to run around with the other dogs. One time, however,

I almost couldn't get him to come back to me; I should have let him get to know me better before unleashing him. Then later Harry went to live temporarily with Tim until I could ask the rental house owner if I could have a dog and pig as residents. Initially, the owner granted permission for Bonnie before I moved in; I made the mistake of not informing him about welcoming Harry. Probably suffering from separation anxiety, he managed to escape twice from the backyard of my former home while Tim was at work.

Hungry, dirty, and infested with fleas, Harry returned days later the second time. Having to assume responsibility for his care and safety made Tim more impatient and temperamental. Without telling me about his intention in advance, Tim took him to a Humane Society Shelter, where he was put down because no other single adult or family thought he was adoptable.

Another pig named Bailey and another dog named Bogi were designated would-be babysitter companions for Bonnie while I was at work. Previously I had been on a seven month sick leave from PERS due to my worsening fibromyalgia and lupus conditions. Way too much inactive time for me and I couldn't allow the circumstance to sink me deeper into a pool of depression. Combined with that factor and my separation from Tim motivated me to return to work, though I started working only half-time. I was home in the afternoon, thus allowing me take care of Bonnie, Bailey, and Bogi.

Once again, I made the mistake of introducing Bonnie to two new animals she didn't know and didn't accept in her environment. She showed her resentment too many times by aggressively charging at them, so I decided to keep her in the spare room; Bogi and Bailey in the living room. It was unfortunate that Bogi triggered my asthma attacks. I made the difficult decision to take him to the Humane Society. I found out that he was adopted the next day. Tim told me he saw him in Gresham; I saw him too.

Marital separation didn't prevent us from taking long walks with our animals (except incapacitated Bonnie couldn't because of a bad knee). Bonnie's overall condition, including depression stemming from the loss of her initial home environment – didn't improve as time passed.

I couldn't tolerate seeing her suffer day after day. I requested my vet to come to my place and put her to sleep. I kept her ashes in a tin box with a photograph of her on top.

I don't know if I made the best decisions about my animal companions in those days because excessive drinking numbed or delayed the dynamics of my grief – the various stages. Only Bailey, my third potbellied pig, was left. He proved to me that he missed Bogi's spunky companionship. I couldn't resist getting a Scottie named Jona (otherwise pronounced "*Yo*-na"). I saw the gesture as a heartfelt tribute to my first fiancee's Icelandic sister whose name was Jona.

Bailey, a Kunekune species, and Jona became best buddies. When I returned from work, they would be a snuggled mix-match on the futon couch – literally piggyback: little brindle Jona lying on top of Bailey's broad white back with random black spots. Situated behind my place was a big grassy field. We entertained ourselves there… Bailey grazing and Jona running circles around him. Jona would often try to engage Bailey in play by running up to him and trying to gently tug on his waddles which were little pieces of fat that hung down from Bailey's jowls. Sometimes, we would go to the nearby park, the same one Tim and I had visited frequently. Even after our separation, I would see him with Clyde and Sisely there.

While as a part-time worker at PERS, and before I got fired, I met Damon Hurdlesen. He became a PERS employee during my extended absence. I would see him in the hallways and shyly whisper "Hello" in passing. I soon came out of my protective shell. By then, I had summoned enough courage to go directly up to him and say, "Hello, my name is Zae. What is yours?"

My curiosity opened the door between us. Sometimes, he would come to my cubicle to give me address changes for disability applicants. He worked in the disability services section and I worked in the retirement services section.

Although my separation from Tim was still painful and filled with regrets, I also felt the pressure of loneliness, lack of human affection, and sexual contact. I needed the right man to fill that vacuum. That's why I decided to give Damon my home phone number. He in turn would call me there in the afternoons. When I was drinking too much I had a tendency to over-confide during our teasing and enticing conversations. For no particular reason I told him I hadn't got pregnant yet, therefore my vagina was tight like a deflowered nineteen year old virgin.

* * *

After my divorce became final, I decided to start an affair with Damon eight days later. Our first encounter happened at my apartment near Gresham. The four-month long wait was worth it. Maybe this was going to be a rebound romance, but from the start it didn't feel that way because I already had a sexual encounter with another guy named David – soon after my separation from Tim. Needy-greedy again, I suppose. Purely sexual. We had no emotional attachment like what would develop between Damon and I.

All of that pent-up anticipation and speculation acted like a lit fuse in dynamite. In the living room, he wasted no time giving me an ardent, lingering kiss that thrust arousal signals throughout my body... age 36, at a sexual peak.

Passion hurried us to the master bedroom, where we wasted no time stripping to bare skin – tanned paleness against African American blackness. Amazement mixed with historical curiosity telegraphed from my stare. He was well endowed for serious lovemaking; a gorgeous entity with sparkling deep brown eyes and sensuous, luscious lips.

What happened next was like an imprisoned dream broken from chains and seeking the right direction to fulfill its single-minded purpose: experimental sex in various positions, culminating in hardcore, multiple climaxes I hadn't experienced before. A fantastic first encounter with a new hunk.

I remember, in the beginning of our relationship, how his soulful eyes glowed whenever he gazed into my eyes. Especially after our first intimate encounter, when I held his face in my hands and whispered, "Beautiful brown-eyed man."

Our official first date occurred at a popular Mexican restaurant. I asked him why he never married; I assumed that was the case because I didn't see the tell-tale imprint of a once worn wedding band.

He failed to hold back a cocky grin. "Too many women." He shrugged, as it were the most appropriate excuse.

Oh crap! I wanted to shout. His response was turning me off. I was just another notch on his penis, another easy piece of pleasure. Yet, after seeing him for three months, I felt certain I was in love with him. And you're saying, "poor girl… another round of *a hard head makes a sore butt syndrome.*"

The figurative bombshell of truth was exposed when one of my trusted co-workers informed me that Damon was still married. The wedding band on his finger had always been present while he was on the job, but somehow my attention wasn't focused on it so much – even when he passed my cubicle or entered it. Was I wearing blinders the whole time? The revelation didn't stop me from wanting more of Damon Hurdlesen, from loving him, from having a possible future with him. Underneath, I was disappointed, and I started drinking more.

Finally, in June 1998, I went into a detox program for my alcoholism. I called Damon from the treatment center in the Cedar Hills community and asked him to come visit me, but not once did he honor my request. While I was in treatment, I met dark-haired, hazel-eyed Sharisse. She was likable, approachable, attractive with exotic looking features reminiscent of Brazilian ancestry. Our chemistry gelled and we started a friendship. At some point, I confided to her about Damon and how he had asked me if I would be willing to engage in a threesome: me, him, and another woman. Was she interested in being a participant? Had she participated in one before? Her responses were "no and no."

Foxy Sharisse pretended that she was single and tried to hit on a few of the guys in our treatment program. The truth jumped out of the box at the treatment program when she received a bouquet of flowers from her husband, whom she was supposedly separated from, on their wedding anniversary.

As I would learn later, she was skilled at deceit and convincing you of her untruths. For example, she told me she had earned a B.S. degree in psychology; instead, that degree was in education. She even earned a master's degree in education, but never worked as a substitute teacher. She further proclaimed to be a housewife, but never cooked or cleaned much. She was too busy doing drugs, both street and prescription, plus alcohol.

After treatment sessions, Sharisse and I would attend AA meetings together and laugh simultaneously about familiar stories of drunkenness. We also went out dancing at the Grand Cafe near MLK Boulevard. We both were supposed to be SOBER. One particular night, however, I surmised she had relapsed and was driving while intoxicated... in a frenzy panic to find her purse. I offered her assistance by searching under her driver's seat. That's where I found the purse and half a fifth of vodka. I didn't confront her – perhaps I should have – but I didn't want to assume the worst and judge her.

Because of my growing social networking with Sharisse and Damon, she was eager to meet him. Each of us agreed to meet for weekend dancing at the Grand Cafe. Before she arrived at my apartment, Damon and I had made love. He was already dressed when she knocked on the front door. I heard their brief conversation with hints of flirtation.

"Welcome," Damon said.

"Well, we finally meet." Sharisse chuckled. "About time, right?"

"Better late than never. No adventure if you miss the cruise ship."

She chuckled again. "Tell me all about it."

"You should be on the cover of a magazine, sweetheart."

"Me? Get real, Damon. That's the first time any man has ventured there."

"No kidding about it."

There was a pause between them.

Then Sharisse asked, "Where's our party girl?"

"Master bedroom."

"Cool. Excuse me, sir."

I was still naked when Sharisse, without knocking, opened the door.

"My god. You have the body of a goddess!" she gushed, dramatically. She was over-emphasizing the truth.

I was in shape, though, from running eight miles at Glendover Park three to four times a week, helping me to lose 20 pounds since I first met Damon. My belly was a suitable female sculptured six-pack. My arms and legs were firm and muscular. (No conceited ego intended, but since preteen years, I always had ample thighs, sturdy ankles, and a shapely round butt.) I was 123 pounds and size two in over-all wear of clothing.

Now I was wearing my cute little eggplant-colored skirt and jacket with an iridescent blue-green with eggplant colored long-sleeved blouse. Sharisse was wearing a blue-green-cream colored crew neck sweater with blue jeans. The sweater highlighted her ample augmented breasts. More than a few times, I caught Damon's eyes focused on the unnaturalness, but her butt, too, was like mine but fuller.

We arrived by Damon's jeep to the Grand Cafe, which was buzzing with party-goers crowding the dance floor. You could smell the admixture of body sweat, perfume, and cologne. I wasn't drinking at the time, but I believe Sharisse was in another relapse phase. She and Damon joined the dancers and as quick as you could snap your fingers, they were bumping and grinding into each other – as if in a preparatory mating ritual: one-way oral sex.

Naturally, I was pissed off because he seemed to desire her more than me. Besides, they weren't as well acquainted. Their dirty dancing bothered me too. Later, the three of us danced together, but he wouldn't dance alone just with me. Okay. I admit I was jealous and wanted Damon all to myself. Otherwise, I didn't consider myself a typical jealous person.

Much later, I returned to the dance floor and danced by myself. A drunk male stranger asked me to dance and I refused. Talk about irony: his drunkenness turned me off but how many people had I turned off when I was sloppy drunk? He continued pestering me… coaxing, putting his hands on my shoulders and back and trying to force me to the center of the group of dancers.

Whenever I danced, I liked to have personal space and not be squashed amongst others, but traveling across the dance floor or on the edges where I could move more freely.

The same drunk asked me to smile and I said, "I'll smile IF I want to; I'm an independent woman!" He sulked away. I resumed dancing as my own partner.

On the return trip to home in Damon's jeep, I sat in the front passenger seat while holding his hand. Sharisse sat in the back. I noticed them taking sneaky peeks at each other through the rear view mirror.

When we drove up to my apartment, Damon was still looking in his rear view mirror, focusing his attention on Sharisse. Then he suddenly turned around and gave me a peck on the lips.

When we entered my apartment to socialize for a little while, I think Damon wanted a threesome with Sharisse and I, but that didn't happen. In the end, I said goodbye to them; they said it to each other before taking separate paths in their cars.

Consequently, since that night, Damon stopped calling me. I told Sharisse about that situation. She admitted the truth: she and Damon were in a relationship. How was she expecting me to react by telling me the joy she got from the way he held her when they went out to a restaurant? Was that another lie, also?

It was true Sharisse was doing street drugs and going to a methadone clinic but bought additional methadone outside the clinic. She, like others, was seeking the ultimate high. She was getting it through sex and drugs, but pretending she and Damon weren't having sex. One time she called me and said that she and Damon were spending hours and hours together, though she never admitted to having sex. I knew that was another lie. I wasn't so mentally wounded, causing me to be blind *and* stupid.

My friendship with Damon was on the verge of ending. We had shared special times, and now I no longer saw him. I talked with him on the phone, but I later learned that Sharisse didn't want him to even talk with me. She was claiming him as *her* boyfriend and didn't want me to *interfere*. In fact, on my 37th birthday, January 30th, he called me, angrily saying, "Why the hell did you tell Sharisse we were still having a relationship? She broke up with me because of your jealous ass. That ends it for us too. Good-bye!"

My world came crushing down on me again and the emotional devastation re-triggered my dependency on alcohol to escape from the pain, to kill it. I ended up at my friend Gerald's apartment, where we got smashed drinking over a gallon of vodka that day.

Echoes of... a hard head makes a sore butt....

After our second trip to the liquor store, I was climbing out of Gerald's high-rise truck on giant wheels. I was toasted. Somehow, my long winter coat got caught on the interior door handle. I loss what little balance I did have before I fell with my butt up in the air, then landed on my head. Gerald described my injury as "splitting open a melon."

Alcohol saturation deadened my awareness of the large laceration causing blood to spurt all over my clothes. Gerald called 911. When the EMTs were talking with me, I remember slurring my words, "Look, you guys... I don't see w-why... I have to – I don't wanna go to the hospital... Lemme dry out h-here."

Nonsense. The ambulance rushed me to nearby Emanual Hospital. I was still drunk, protesting like a fool. The last thing I remembered the emergency room surgeon saying was *"We're losing her; she's lost too much damn blood!"*

But I survived the ordeal and woke up with stitches going from the middle of my forehead to down the back of my head. The EMTs said it was the largest laceration they had ever seen. Here again, I believe God was watching over me. Still, He wasn't done with me yet.

After that first surgery on the head laceration, a life-threatening blood clot formed. My face was more black and blue and swollen, requiring a second surgery and the injection of 32 staples. From that procedure I got an infection. I was put on antibiotics and re-stitched a final time.

Thoughts of Damon should have been buried far away into my mind, but we started talking again that spring. I felt certain he had patched things up with Sharisse because he never came to visit me. By this time, I was living in SE Portland, off of 52nd and Tenino Street. My cohabitant Nelly was also divorced and the owner of a two-bedroom bungalow. I had to move there because I could no longer afford to pay $625 monthly rent for my two-bedroom rental near Gresham. I was running out of mortgage money from my divorce settlement; I had to withdraw money from my deferred compensation account in order to pay her each month.

Nelly was cool about welcoming Bailey and Jona to live with us. Nelly was a student studying to be a respiratory therapist. She worked part-time in a bakery. We agreed that Bailey, being a pig, should live outside. She had never heard of a pig acclimated to indoor living in a house.

I put a big, thick, plastic hutch outside on the porch for him to sleep in. Because of cold weather conditions, I had a heat lamp arranged over the top of the hutch. I missed the interaction that I used to have with him when I lived near Gresham. Springtime was even too chilly for him to spend much time outdoors. Sometimes, I would go out and snuggle with him under the heat lamp.

Bailey tried to get into the house by chewing on the cat door. We would just see his snout through the slot. I used to sleep with my pet companions on the mattress and box-spring that I had set up in the two-bedroom apartment that we (Bailey, Jona, and I) had lived in before coming to live with Nelly.

In the new place, I cuddled with Jona at night. She was a big comfort though I missed cuddling with Bailey, as well. I was sober and went to AA when I first moved into the Tenino house. I made the mistake of telling Nelly that I was an alcoholic in recovery, and when I began drinking again, she found out and put me on probation as a tenant. Well, I stopped drinking for a while, but I got a second DUII when I mistakenly started drinking again.

I was driving to work and I had drank the night before and that morning. I pulled off the shoulder of the highway when I realized I couldn't drive safely. Later, a two-man police patrol stopped when they saw my car parked on the side of the shoulder. They did sobriety tests on me, but I didn't remember them because I was blacked-out by then, in the backseat of my car. Somehow, I got the car towed back to my house. I stayed sober for a while after that, but one afternoon I was coming back from work, and I discovered that Bailey had escaped from the backyard when I got home. I was frantic when I discovered Bailey missing. I called the shelters and eventually learned that animal control service had captured him. I had to pay a fine because they said he was too big for Portland city limits. Therefore, I had to find him a new home outside of Portland. I contacted my very understanding potbellied breeder and she provided her truck which allowed him to climb onto a ramp attached to the truck's rear end.

Driving my 1972 Chevy Chevelle I followed them. When we arrived at the potbellied pig ranch, my breeder put Bailey in a pen next to his father, basking under a heat lamp. I held Baily, gave him an apple, and said goodbye to him. My kindly breeder said I could come visit him anytime, just let her know ahead of time. Fate dictated a much later visit.

My darn Chevelle's engine broke down and I didn't have enough money to get it repaired. Bailey escaped from Nelly's backyard more easily because she had removed the ribbon of electric fencing, without asking me. So he ended up in the neighbor's yard; the animal control service folks had informed me. I suppose Bailey was seeking greener pastures after having "mowed" down her backyard lawn. Although many years have passed, I'm crying now because of my last visit with him at the breeding farm. I am reminded of the loss of another beloved animal companion.

A not so subtle grief re-triggered my urge to drink alcohol. On top of that, Jona wouldn't eat for weeks because she missed her beloved pig that had been like a puppy. Nelly found out about my relapse when she saw me leave in a taxi for a round trip fare. She was no dummy. She flipped out. She snatched my backpack from me and removed the purchased fifth of vodka. At that point, I didn't know what her intentions were, but I resented her attitude and boldness. What happened to my fifth? Without a single protest word from me, she took it to her bedroom, drank it all over a period of time until the bottle was empty.

Under the circumstances, she turned into an apathetic bitch who demanded I move out. I was faced with another transition during the spring of 1999. Jona stayed with Nelly for two weeks while I stayed with my friends Margie and Stuart.

We had fun watching movies together and smoking pot. Margie talked funny when she was high, as if her head was under water and making her incoherent. Usually, Stuart and I laughed and laughed. One time while I was staying with them, Stuart and I had sex on the couch in the living room of the one bedroom apartment. Maybe thinking my erotic reactions sounded more like a person having a seizure, a sleepy Margie rushed from her bedroom and witnessed reality. She was a good sport about it; we even laughed and shrugged it off.

Another time, while I was already drunk, I left the apartment to buy more wine. When I returned, Stuart took the bottle away from me, saying, "You've had enough to drink." He clamped fingers on my elbow and his other hand pushed me into Margie's bedroom. "You're a mess. Stay in here and sober up."

Yet another transition but one leading to life in a so-called "Northeast inner-city hood" with a reputation for drug dealing, prostitution, domestic violence, and drive-by shootings. Never to receive approval by the staff of *Good Housekeeping* Magazine, I rented a cheap studio apartment for $365 monthly.

It was located off of NE Grand and NE Dekum. I will stop here and spare you the awful details of interior layout and the variety of creepy-crawly pests.

Damon and Sharisse still had a relationship but he found out where I was living and paid me visits. The seasoned womanizer hadn't changed a bit; he was determined to rekindle the sexual passion we once shared. Somehow, he persuaded me to indulge in a threesome with a straight female friend who used her talents on me. However, I was not a typical, full-fledged lesbian.

Either I was naturally oversexed or my use of alcohol was the greatest stimulant for my particular libido. The sexual cravings were like a monumental itch that nothing could soothe or stop. My inhibitions would fly out the window. Especially, after I got sufficiently drunk, I would strike up conversations with half-way attractive male strangers I discovered on bus routes. Those potentially dangerous encounters left me more depressed than satisfied… after I sobered down to reality. Most of the time, I wouldn't remember what had occurred, who the man was, and where it happened.

Each time, I survived from being physically unscathed and I thank The Almighty for that degree of protection. Amen.

A drug dealer gunslinger named Avril visited my Dekum address whenever another drug dealer, named Richard, was present. I gave her permission to smoke crack on several occasions. Here again, my inhibitions had free will to do whatever when it came to sex. Avril and I got naked, in anticipation of receiving more crack for future distribution at my place and for personal use. Because of the former, I should have received more crack.

Didn't take long for particular crack-smoking cliques to discover that my place was safe enough for indulgence seven days a week. Thus began the circus-like, zombie atmosphere; I seemed unafraid of consequences.

More binge drinking...

More crack cocaine smoking...

More uninhibited sex with multiple partners...

Threats on my life...

Theft of personal property...

Enough was enough, I finally told myself, but before I ended my association with those other crack addicts, they helped me move my stuff to a storage unit, right next door to the apartment in SW Portland (The Grail) that I moved to after being in NE Portland. For their assistance, they demanded crack, of course. When the new apartment became available, they helped move the property from the storage space.

The Grail was located next to a restaurant and bar named The Boom Boom Room. I never ventured into the bar; I preferred to drink alone and not in a public place. I did go to get takeout hot and sour soup a couple of times at the restaurant. There was also an adult entertainment business situated next to it. Lack of curiosity prevented me from going inside. My adult entertainment consisted of trying my luck picking up strange men, more so when I was drunk. I suppose I made myself a potential target for enterprising serial killers. Oregon had a few such infamous types during this time period. And if I were born with three vaginas, I also suppose each one would be occupied with sex.

No woman should ever be that horny (man either). Sometimes, you just gotta add a hardy dose of humor to reduce the pain of truth.

My triumph over ending my crack smoking addiction didn't make front page news in the *Oregonian* Newspaper. Our minds and bodies have limits when it comes to devastating pain making you wish you were dead; making you wish you could transport yourself to another planet in order to escape to a brand new reality – making you wish you were never born.

My *new* strength was tested when drug dealer Richard visited me, after Avril gave him my then current address. He came for a "preview" which meant he just wanted to see me naked while he alternate between masturbating and smoking crack. You'd have to see it for yourself to believe it.

I didn't have a pipe, so he let me borrow the one he used to smoke marijuana. He left me with that pipe, some filters, a stingy amount of crack I could smoke on my own and a porn DVD.

I put on a Marvin Gaye song entitled *"What's Going On?"* before I settled on my sofa. The broken pieces of crack were secured in a clear baggie. I suspected the sealed quality would be downgraded to a 2 or 4 – a baking soda trickster special... just enough to give you a slight tingle and boost your appetite for more and more and....

I stared so hard at the cause of my misery and cash money reducer that the sweat from my forehead dripped over my eyelids, trembling lips, chin, and spotted the chest area of my workout T-shirt from my college days in Seattle. Other aspects of my past life unwound in my mind as the master of R&B soul music belted out his evocative lyrics. I swear those tidbits of crack seemed to be grinning at me, their mini arms pumping like sideline cheerleaders waiting for their team players to make the final winning score.

The more I stared and sweat dripped, the more my mouth and tongue felt like a worn carpet. My eyes shifted to the marijuana pipe and filters. Next to the pipe was a Bic lighter. I struggled to swallow but no saliva went down. I used my forearm to clear the sweat.

I scooted closer to the coffee table, already feeling the utopic rush of the drug. *Do you really want to continue being its slave?* I thought. *Why aren't you dead yet, girl?*

Pressure in my head led to throbbing and its annoyance jerked me to my feet. I wanted to dance because Marvin Gaye was still musically jamming the words that seemed to illuminate my small environment.

I then began pacing back and forth, my focus only on the dull white pebbly destroyer of lives, careers, properties, reputations, integrities, incomes, freedom of choices.

Suddenly, I stopped pacing. I remember my tense shoulders sagging with the exhalation of a big sigh. So strange how one half of me felt weak, while the other half felt mighty – I saw it as hope washing over me like a baptismal ceremony.

A smile flushed my cheeks as I bent, lifted the baggie, and carried it to the bathroom.

Tears blinded my vision but I was beyond caring as I raised the opened baggie and angled it downward. Still smiling, I watched the poison tumble into the toilet and be forever destroyed soon after I gripped the flush handle.

"Thank you, Lord. Never again as long as I live." I flushed the toilet a second time. I stared at the twirling water. "No more a slave. I promise."

The second time Richard arrived I gave him back the porn DVD, marijuana pipe, and filters. After that, he wanted us to smoke crack and freak out again. I didn't explain to him the transition I had experienced. I made it absolutely clear to him that I didn't want him around me anymore and never try to persuade me to use crack again. Apparently, he felt the seriousness of my vibes and they kept him away... ending his visits. No regrets.

Now I was becoming more like the Zae Rankin of my teen years and young adulthood, but I still had to defeat my dependency on wine and vodka. I didn't grow up with addicts. My parents rarely ever drank; unopened wine bottles would sit in the refrigerator for months. Once in a while my dad would have a beer with the German man whose dissertation he was editing.

Value-wise, I grew up in the environment of a somewhat liberal Methodist Church. To the contrary, what disturbed me the most was when my parents had blow-you-out-the-water arguments and physical challenges during my childhood.

Why couldn't they get their act together sooner? Why was I always the center of their conflicts? And would the marital storms cease when I'd set sail to go to college? For sure, the "horrors" of my past broadcast in memoir form would arouse their emotions: pity, fear, loathing, wonder, speculation, disbelief, other.

CHAPTER TEN

FIGHTING FOR LASTING REDEMPTION

Those first few days after I cold-quit smoking crack were tough on my residual cravings or what I would describe as "ghost feelings" in my central nervous system that had gotten so well-acquainted with the white poison. Unlike marijuana smoking that gives the user an enhanced appetite, crack had diminished my appetite for food, thus causing me to lose weight. I was down to 125 pounds compared to my pre-crack weight of 160 pounds. I probably looked emaciated, if my parents were present to see my body. I suppose I was one of the lucky ones because other crack addicts I knew looked like walking skeletons with vacant bulging eyes.

The desire to run for purely exercise returned. I wanted to reclaim my stamina and physical strength and sense of peace through motion. First, though, I broke in a new pair of Nike running shoes by walking five miles from my neighborhood during weekends. Spring had already arrived and I was still harassed by allergens that always aggravated my asthma. Not much later, I became bolder by walking ten miles. My feet got punished from the ordeal, but the punishment sure boosted my morale, perseverance, and resilience. Made me smile more. Gave me hope for a brighter future. All I had to do was be faithful to the plan God had intended me to follow.

The year 1999. The approaching New Millennium was the talk and focus of the world. Humans from all walks of life and doomsday theorists were predicting the end of civilization after December 31st. Dormant volcanoes would erupt at the same time. Meteors three times the size of Texas were expected to pulverize the United States. Sudden sea levels would drown all of Florida. Riots and murders like never before in history. Gun shop owners couldn't keep up with demands, as well as food supply chains.

I had fears of my own, but I wasn't overly fearful of death. Besides, I already had several near-death experiences attributed to both medical issues and suicide. My parents got sucked up in all the doomsday predictions and considered moving to a safer country less vulnerable than America. During one telephone conversation with my mom, I told her they could run as fast as a sprinter in the Olympics but they wouldn't be able to hide like notorious bank robbers fleeing to South America.

Maybe you cheered for me on the day I finally kicked the crack smoking addiction. Good for you if you did. However, my fibromyalgia and lupus diagnoses still plagued my life. I still drank too much vodka, as if it were a natural medicine and cure-all. AA meetings weren't advantageous the way I had hoped. I was happy for the graduation success of those few AA attendees I had befriended. I had heard through the grapevine that Sharisse's alcohol addiction was worsening and damage to her liver was severe enough to require her hospitalization for a month.

What I did next was downright stupid and unforgivable. A ten-year old child would have been better behaved.

A week before the New Year of 2000 would begin, I woke up that Monday morning with an insatiable thirst for vodka. I had half a fifth on standby in the kitchen cabinet. Didn't help matters that I ignored eating breakfast – anything to lessen the void in my stomach. Last night's Taco Bell tacos were already digested. My twisted mentality told me to hide the vodka bottle in my backpack and take it with me to work.

I was afforded some degree of privacy in my PERS cubicle. I had only a five-hour work shift. Two hours later, I took my first fifteen minute break. When in-house foot traffic had ceased, I drank from the bottle. The liquid burned in my empty stomach but I knew the pain would vanish soon and the familiar initial high would kick in.

As I was about to sneak the vodka bottle from the backpack again, a long term co-worker knocked on the glass partition then stood in the doorway. Her unexpected appearance might have made me look like I just swallowed an ostrich egg.

Louise gave me a funny look when she asked, "You think the world is really going to end within the next five days?"

I knew I was busted when she started sniffing but wasn't sure her nose was telling her correctly. I shrugged, hoping she'd leave right away. "I seriously doubt it. Maybe in the next 100,000 years. Humans don't deserve Earth anymore."

"Hmmm... I agree with the last part." She paused before she took a step closer. "Do you smell that?"

"Smell what?" I frowned at her while trying to play dumb.

"I thought I smelled alcohol."

"Really?"

"Well, I thought so." Louise checked her watch. "I better get moving. My break time is over." She wiggled her fingers. "See you tomorrow, Zae."

"Sure thing. Take care." I let out a huge sigh of relief, feeling grateful for her departure. If her suspicion had grown deeper, I was prepared to tell her a lie: *Oh that. I got a paper cut on my finger and I used rubbing alcohol on it....*

There are three types of drunks:

(A) Sociable, funny, life of the party.

(B) Sloppy, staggering, incoherent.

(C) Unconscious, dead to the world, snoring up a storm.

After having consumed the equivalent of 1/3 worth of the fifth, I turned myself into the C type drunk, at my desk. I was discovered by frightened co-workers, with my head weighted sideways down on the desktop. My mouth was agape, allowing saliva to drool under my left cheek and chin. The smell of vodka was evident this time because I had spilled some on my backpack and failed to re-screw the cap on the fifth. A supervisor was summoned. She assessed the situation then called 911. An emergency truck rushed me to the nearest hospital. My stomach was pumped. I was given anti-nausea medication. Took me hours to reach sobriety. I was released, with my life intact. I felt I could never face my co-workers again. The shame. The hurt. The fear. I already knew a hammer-like blow of punishment was coming.

To my surprise, I was placed on a probationary period of four months from PERS and policy dictated that I get better treatment for alcoholism. I failed at the second chance because of a non-alcohol related incident that made me not report for work for three days. Near the end of December I received an employment termination letter to my address. Was it enough of a wakeup call?

What followed was a series of short-term employment opportunities and I was a telemarketer each time.

Those in-between years (2001-2005) trudged along like a winding lazy river. The world, though getting more dangerous, anti-political, and unpredictable, was still intact. Crack was no longer popular because of deterrent factors like stiffer legal penalties, major DEA busts of kingpins and cartels, and more prison construction. Those consequences made me happy. For me, crack was another personal history lesson I would not forget.

The arrival of January 2009. That date marked the granting of my Social Security Disability status that I had been waiting to receive for six years. What a timely blessing! An attorney had aided me in the process. I was riddled with so much severe pain that I couldn't sit for even the duration of a five-hour shift at Rockwell Research conducting surveys over the phone for Banfield Pet Hospital.

During the last three years of my residency at The Grail apartment complex, I managed to pull off another miracle-like feat: I stayed sober and stuck with the challenge for a total of six years... from 2006 to 2012. I tested my level of tolerance by drinking a glass of wine once in a while, without reverting to my addiction levels. Even now as I vividly reflect, I had believed there was no ending my alcohol abuse.

While I waited for a lump sum payment, my dear mom paid my rent and gave me an extra $100 a month for other expenses. I received food stamp assistance because of my disability.

What prompted me to finally remain sober was that my doctor prescribed Vicodin and Baclofen, a relaxant for pain. Also, the last time I drank before consuming the new medicines, I had had two glasses of wine – not understanding why I needed to guzzle one after the other. How I vomited looked as violent as a prize fighter's fist slamming full force into an opponent's abdomen.

That instance of stupidity worked like a charm. I had had ENOUGH... I didn't want to go out and buy a fifth of vodka, like I normally would have done, and repeat the vicious cycle. I prayed for strength. Now that I had something to help alleviate my severe pain, I found the will to stay sober. The Vicodin worked for a while but wasn't strong enough, so my doctor switched me to Methadone for a short time then prescribed Morphine which wasn't as strong as the Methadone but was much safer.

CHAPTER ELEVEN

BIG HOPE ARRIVES ON FOUR LEGS – SOLAS

No one on our planet can even guess how many human lives have been changed for betterment by other humans, companion animals, poems, books, movies, concerts, architecture, hobbies, recipes, education, etc., etc. Not yet have scientific studies been conducted to explore the cause and effect of such fateful turnarounds. Still, I must ask the obvious question: What factors play a role to make those transitions toward betterment happen?

My love and respect for my companion animals is well documented in this memoir. Each in their own animal insight rescued me from a deeper hole of degradation, loneliness, hardship, and the toxicity of self-pity. Without a doubt in my mind, I know I would have perished before I turned 35. Many times their affection, allegiance and attentiveness seemed more potent than what I might have received from relatives and intimate friends.

Medium-size dogs and adorable pot bellied pigs had (one was named Bailey and his character was multi-faceted) always been my favorites since my childhood. None of my former crack buddies had special attachments to pet companions like I did, all inspired by summertime vacations on my grandparents Double Eagle Farm near Vale, Oregon.

My will power and determination helped to defeat two addictions that had enslaved me for years, but I still suffer from different kinds of pain caused by that unsolved hit and run crime. And of course, the threat of asthma is always a shadow over my otherwise healthy body.

The other major thing that happened in my life, helping me to maintain sobriety, was the arrival of a new dog I named Solas, a Scottish name that means solace (dictionary definition: peace, tranquility, restfulness). In April 2009, he was six months old when I obtained him from a breeder – four months after I moved to public housing at the Ruth Haefner Plaza Apartments in SW Portland.

Solas was a darling Maltipoo (Maltese/toy poodle mix). The first week he was under my care I stayed with my friend Laura who resided as an on-site manager at The Grail. Housing authority policy dictated that he couldn't become a pet resident of my subsidized apartment until after he was neutered. That was accomplished.

Solas and I got better acquainted as the days and weeks turned into months. When we weren't outside taking beneficial walks, we relaxed on the couch long enough to accommodate five human visitors. We had an entertainment ritual: Every morning we would watch the TV series *Matlock, In The Heat of the Night,* and *Perry Mason*.

He was cool enough in attitude to watch movements on the screen and listen to the dialogues of actors; the same observations for commercials featuring cats and dogs – whether real or animated. He wasn't an excessive barker like other breeds. His amiable personality was a plus.

I taught him how to fetch an orange fluorescent rubber ball that first week of his companionship at the apartment plaza. Afterward, he got bored of the game and would no longer participate. I couldn't understand why. I didn't force the issue but it was another method to ensure his overall health through consistent vigorous exercise.

Another seeming behavioral issue I discovered was his disdain for pet toys, except my decades-old collection of stuffed animals. Without me being aware, he was like a sneaky thief in the night digging his teeth into their sacrificial bodies and ripping off their innocent plastic eyes.

Solas was a fanatic about adventuring in the outdoors, especially long walks along scenic, tree-lined SW Beaverton-Hillsdale Highway or the expansive dog park on the same route – just a five-minute Trimet bus ride. He would romp with other over-energized dogs of varying sizes and personalities... around the path over the creek... up and down gentle grassy knolls. He must've ran a good four to six miles in the hour we stayed at the park each day. Besides being athletic, he was a snuggler, at least in his first years. Later, he became more independent; didn't want me to secure him in his carrier. On one occasion, while he was secured in my arms, he tried to bite me when I was situating him to be placed into the topside of the carrier. So I let him enter by himself, through the front side.

Maltipoo Solas gave me wonderful peace and joy – I swear, everyday with him was filled with the kind of happiness non-pet companion owners can't fully understand. Such companions can be like sounding boards collecting words of weariness, doubts, suspicions, hope, humor, fear, optimism – without verbal feedback humans would otherwise provide, while showering your pet companion with affection and hugs and "I love yous". Imagine a world where humans respected the power of silence, of listening attentively.

My four-legged friend ate people's food his first six months of life – before I brought him to his new home with me. That diet seemed to have spoiled him because I tried several top graded dog foods including freeze dried raw food, but he still preferred *baked chicken breast*. I also fed him the "gospel" bird, especially after he suffered a bout of pancreatitis from fatty dog food. I also gave him multivitamins manufactured by Chewy.

Solas' breed was characteristic of a thick hair coat that was wavy and sometimes matted. Those factors required me to get him professionally groomed every five to seven weeks, more so in the summertime. If I was unable to secure a grooming appointment or my monthly budget couldn't afford the expense, I would arrange cloth ice packs for him to lay on and water spritz his body several times a day to keep him cool. I also bought an air conditioner but when the temperature rose to 115 degrees one summer, the air conditioner only cooled the living room to 85 degrees. He couldn't tolerate any heat over 70 degrees.

I remember when my friend Marti stayed overnight at my apartment one particular time and he affectionately rested his head on her forehead. So cute.(Whenever she came to visit, the first thing Solas would do is jump in her lap and snuggle down.) Marti had a nightmare that night. To the rescue like the late-50s box office German Shepherd hero Rin Tin Tin came my Solas. Sensing her distress, he jumped on her stomach, licked her face, whimpered and barked to wake her up. Similarly, he rescued me whenever I had nightmares in bed.

His regular sleeping quarters was under a square wooden table situated in the right corner of the bedroom, adjacent to the queen-size bed. Familiar visitors knew that setup was Solas' "apartment". Sometimes during the day he would go there to... "canine meditate".

My bedroom TV had a built-in VCR unit. Remember the original England-produced early 1960s TV series *Dark Shadows*, then was transported to a reunion version to America? I feel blessed to still have the entire whopping collection of VHS tapes. Usually takes me almost a year to re-watch them all. Well, the spooky, vampire cast of characters (in particular the irrepressible character Barnabas) sometimes would watch us sleeping before show's ending.

During the first few years with Solas I cleaned his paws every day because he enjoyed roaming about in the broad backyard of the Ruth Haefner Plaza, where other residents exercised and relieved their pet companions or registered service dogs. An accumulation of fur encircled his butt, so I cleaned that area from having dried poop balls multiply. An owner's maintenance duties are essential for a continuing span of good health. He often had to have his ears cleaned due to intrusive hair which caused many of his ear infections. At first, I was able to apply ear drops, but after a while, he began to bite when I tried. The task was more suitable for a vet who put a clever concave muzzle cone around his head to prevent his biting. After the administering of the ear drops, he would be scheduled back a week later for more treatment. I later determined that his biting episodes was attributed to him not feeling well.

A close call catastrophe. I also remember the day when we returned from a lengthy walk on a trail on the hill above Beaverton-Hillsdale

Highway. We were stepping closer to the ground floor sliding door of the lobby entrance of the apartment complex. For whatever reason, Solas got spooked, and broke free from his collar and leash. I kept calling his name – "SOLAS... SOLAS! COME BACK! MOMMIE NEEDS YOU!" as he raced toward coming-and-going dangerous lanes of traffic.

Some motorists, also panicky, attempted to stop for us, but another motorist ran over Solas' left front paw. I was screaming for help. He was yelping in pain, yet still managed to allude my running approach. He got lost somewhere on the hill. I searched and searched for hours and so did motorist companion Laura. We couldn't find poor Solas.

I gave a favorite photo of him, with my cell phone number scribbled on it, to a nursing home receptionist, in case she or others spotted him. My good friend Marti stayed over to comfort me with hugs and verbal reassurances, but my nerves felt rubbed raw I was so upset and restless.

His disappearance and injury drove me out of bed numerous times in the late night time hours... going downstairs on the elevator, exiting the plaza lobby, staring across the illuminated highway, half-expecting to discover him in the middle of it – *dead*.

Either what happened next was pure luck or divine intervention.

The next morning, that nursing receptionist (a dog lover who owned a Jack Russell terrier) phoned me and said he was spotted at the top of the hill, and he was limping. I almost shouted for joy, but I said, with relief in my voice, "Hold on, I'll be right there. I just live across the street. Can you stay with him?"

Snatching up his collar and leash off the floor, I dashed to the elevators.

Hurry... damnit! Hurry!

Seemed to have taken an eternity to reach ground floor from fourth floor.

I was shaking like a wind-blown leaf and teary-eyed when I ran across the highway. Unbelievable! My god...there he was! I found him sitting forlornly in a ditch, his fur coated with musty wetness. I scooped him up in my arms and brought him home. No other dog owner in the entire world that day felt hugely elated and thankful – that was my selfish point of view.

I took him to my vet and he examined Solas and concluded he suffered a broken toe which had to mend on its own. Pain medication was then prescribed.

Another scary moment was when I lost Solas in the off-leash area of the dog park. Initial rounds of thunder frightened him. He escaped from me and hustled off into the dense area of shade trees. I told other park visitors that I had lost him and they assisted in my search. Pet companion owners there were stubbornly loyal to all the well behaved breeds present.

One considerate and kind citizen found Solas. He was waiting at the Route 54 Trimet bus stop, chilling, as if he didn't have a care in the world. He was equally cool-headed when I picked him up in my arms and brought him back to our home. Once again, I was very grateful and thought that his dog common sense (if there is such a thing) motivated him to wait for me there. That section of Beaverton-Hillsdale Highway is exceptionally dangerous during various daytime periods. A four lane crash zone for motorists traveling either way for miles.

In 2017, when Solas turned eight, I was no longer able to walk him due to bone parts of my right knee rubbing against each other; the cartilage was completely worn down. Arthritis had settled in too. I was crippled, barely able to walk across the highway to the nearest bus stop. My friend Crissy was kind enough to take Solas out for a two-mile round trip walk everyday for two years. I felt so blessed to have a loyal Crissy in my corner. You'll never be forgotten, dearest Crissy.

In 2019, my knee surgery was performed – a successful procedure projected to last for many years. Solas was ten and he stayed in a place named Safe Journey Dog Boarding. Dog clients were clustered together on the first floor and not in separate kennel cages. I stayed in the hospital for four days and three and a half weeks in the nursing home after the surgery. Meanwhile, Solas was making new dog friends. He formed a pack with two other small dogs and, like a disciplinarian drill sergeant, kept the wayward puppies in their place. And like a worried mother hen, I phoned the boarding business everyday to hear from staff how he was doing. My worry focused on to what degree he would miss his new dog friends once I brought him back home. Thankfully, he adjusted. Although I knew he loved the companionship of other dogs, we were no longer dog park attendees.

Chrissy, who had come to love Solas and their daily walks to the store, continued to be our walking companion. About two years later, though, Chrissy ended up in a nursing home where she died. Her death was a crushing blow to me and that factor made me both miserable and more dependent on Solas for comfort and regaining my emotional stability. Took awhile for me to lessen my degree of grief. I couldn't speak for Solas, but I felt he grieved in his own way too. During that difficult time for us, an unlikely stranger entered our lives. Was it another case of Roulette Fate?

Solas' life became more medically complicated due to his injured paw and aging. Even when he would lay down in one of the two elevators, he expressed the pain he felt before we exited the plaza. He whimpered when we returned from visiting the spacious back yard. Arthritis was attacking him, too, in that injured paw. I took him to my vet who subscribed gabapentin for pain and trazadone for his moodiness and biting.

In 2013, when Solas was four, I self-published a poetry book titled *Journeys of The Heart and Dedication Poems* (under my real name) and included the following poem for him:

<u>For Solas</u>

Little pitter-patter
whining softly
jumping high
into the sky
thinking only of his walk
at the dog park.

Sniffing here and
sniffing there –

checking messages
from other dogs.

I know God
sent you to me,
full of a love so
pure and free.

Oh what joy, what
comfort, what peace
my little dog brings
to me such release.

Wet nose and salty tongue,
midnight blue eyes,
curly champagne hair,
a permanent reminder
of your loveliness.

My little Maltipoo
makes me new,
full with the grace
of a prince, he jumps
up in your lap
for a scratch.

After nightmare,
he is there
in my arms
licking me as if to say,
"Mommy, tomorrow is
a brand new day."

It's good to be curious about other people, places, and things you aren't familiar with. Doing so could open up the door leading to wonderful surprises and outcomes. Could lead to disastrous outcomes too. Roll your dice, ladies and gentlemen, and hope you hit a lucky No.7 payoff.

Nowadays, the Ruth Haefner Plaza Apartments – approximately age 60 – reminds me of a sloppy fat spinster who has guzzled too many Miller beers, with runs in her black stockings, and brown-stained false teeth showcased in a Mason jar. The HUD-owned property is surrounded by eclectic neighbors, from working-class to middle-class to upper-class. A mini united nations of residents reside in apartments and homes. You will find a pleasant atmosphere of peace and less stressing over rampant crime and other foolishness in our neighborhoods. Car accidents, however, are more predictable.

It was there that my curiosity was focused on one of our tenants who would exit in the morning then return in the evening to his apartment. He usually carried a unique looking spring green colored carrying case an artist might use to transport art. I was an avid painter and my favorite style of painting was abstraction. You could go deeply adventurous with it or be as subtle as a ripple reflection in a pool of water. Like I still do, I mostly painted with oils and acrylics. The activity is fun, relaxing, and keeps me focused.

I later heard his name mentioned by another resident and she told someone else that he was visual artist Raymond Alexander, who was quiet, not overly sociable, and respectful of other residents' privacy. He was a mystery who sustained my curiosity and I wanted to learn more facts about his background.

But before Raymond became a meaningful friend much later, my life was running only on six out of eight cylinders, so to speak, during the winter of 2012, because I was ingesting 30 pills everyday. Some of the more potent drugs (in particular high doses of morphine) did a whammy on my brain: I started hearing voices that really didn't exist in my apartment and outside. I saw images of strange looking people and objects that really didn't exist.

Those aftereffects are tame compared to what happened to me in the spring of 2001. I was staying at a motel on Barbur Boulevard, not far from the apartment complex called The Grail, where I would find my next long-term home. I was waiting for my apartment to be ready to move into in about two weeks. I had taken out my PERS retirement because I had no other source of income. There was a penalty for early withdrawal and I wouldn't receive the double amount at retirement age. But I was desperate to get out of Johnnie Rahwaye's place.

I had Avril, one of my crack buddies, and her male friends help me move my stuff, in the meantime, to a storage unit right next to the new apartment. Of course, I paid them in crack.

After finally moving into the Grail, I began hearing voices condemning me: *"That woman has been giving methadone to the manager and we are going to make sure she goes to jail."* I was so desperately afraid of going back to jail because of my first near-death experience there due to my asthma attack. That assumed verbal taunting inspired me to seek suicide as a possible solution to end all of my problems. I even had a hallucination about all of my loved ones standing around me at Trimet's SW Barbur Transit Center, chanting, *"Suicide is your best option… suicide is your best option…"*

Like in a trance, I walked from the transit center to the nearest restaurant and asked for a cup of water to wash down the morphine pills. I consumed them while I was sitting on a stone wall situated from the sidewalk and across from the restaurant.

I returned to my apartment and called my closest friends, Sharisse and Damon and my mom and said my "good-byes." Sharisse took my fatalistic tone seriously because of my past behaviors, like when I asked one of the Safeway checkers to call Sharisse to come pick me up and I had with me an empty suitcase. Thanks to her, I am still alive to share my story.

She called 911. Soon thereafter, paramedics forced my apartment door open and found me unconscious on the bedroom floor, completely naked. I was rushed to the hospital, where nurses put me on a respirator or iron lung machine to help with the suppressed breathing the high dosage of morphine had caused. It was pumped out of me – the equivalent of 60 pills.

Because I was unconscious, I think I was a patient in the ICU for a few days. The first time I remember being at the hospital was when I woke up in the iron lung and said, "Get me out of here... it's all redness and flames!" Like a vision of hell exists. The nurse responded, "We'll remove you as soon as you can clearly focus on the room."

Afterwards, I went into Respite Care to help me adjust to the real world after my suicide attempt. In Respite Care I met my now good friend Marti, whom I first introduced myself to while I smoked a cigarette on the patio. I gave her a shoulder rub. It was at that point that she considered me a person worthy of staying in contact with. We exchanged phone numbers. She has turned out to be a true and honest friend.

I finally got home. I vowed to never try suicide again, but I was still hearing voices until my first years at Ruth Haefner Plaza and was undiagnosed at that time. For example, my dog companion Solas was in his safety carrier and I placed it in to a grocery cart, along with my dresses and high heels.

I took the cart to the outside entrance of the plaza, thinking that Damon was going to pick me up and take me out dancing in my gold sequined dress and sparkly gold high heels.

My unjustified appearance was unrealistic and troublesome. Same as for the time when I thought I had sleep walked to my neighbor's apartment and proclaimed to Phyliss, "I'm going to *kill* you because you killed Solas by leaving him to *burn* to death by the radiator!" Another hallucinatory lie. I pushed Damon out of my apartment because I thought I heard his jealous wife cussing up a storm and threatening to kick my butt all over Portland.

The last time I had an hallucinatory downfall, which could have jeopardized my safety, I was diagnosed and prescribed schizophrenia medication. What followed was an appointment at the Old Town Clinic on East Burnside Street. Solas accompanied me. I asked staff if Solas could remain in their custody while I committed myself to a week long residency at a psych ward.

I was reaching out for help and thankfully the long-time nurse I had known agreed to take care of him. She welcomed him to her home for a week. Her little dog and him made fast friends.

My psychiatric treatment and out-patient status included ingesting seven milligrams of Haloperidol. Now I was more like a happy camper because my medications were reduced to twelve. I felt so blessed to still be alive!

The more I saw Raymond with his unique carrying case, the more my curiosity grew. What I unfairly thought about was his possible rejection of me for being a woman with multi-racial ethnicity and him being an African-American. Did he feel comfortable being around white females, let alone dating them? I suppose the worse thing that could happen, after a possible introduction initiated by me, would be a rejection via his further distancing attitude of not wanting to be bothered.

One day, though, we were both situated at the Trimet bus stop across from the Ruth Haefner Plaza. It was mid-morning and sunny. This time he didn't have his carrier. I wanted to know was it handmade or manufactured otherwise.

"My name's Zae… Zae Rankin."

"How you doing?"

"I feel okay." I was smiling but he wasn't. He seemed more preoccupied. "When did you become a resident?"

"I'm Raymond." We shook hands. "I moved there in December 2013."

"Are you an artist too?"

"Visual artist."

"That's cool. I'm one. I paint with oils and acrylics."

"I also recycle used manila file folders into various art objects."

"Oh wow. Sounds interesting. Never heard that before." He glanced away from me and saw our bus was heading toward us, just two blocks away."

"A long story how a single file folder changed my direction."

I may have smiled after he told me; I still couldn't imagine something as simple as a file folder having such power over a person's life. I was eager to learn more about that crazy-sounding transition. What I hadn't assumed about him was his past history of drug or alcohol abuse. He didn't seem like a former abuser of either one. He was reasonably attractive with a medium-brown complexion (not the politically popular designated Black associated with Blackness of skin color) several feet short of being six feet even. To me, his two most distinguishing features were his almond shaped brown eyes and wing-like thick mustache. While I became more familiar with him during the coming months and years, he told me that people throughout the years told him he resembled the iconic comedian Richard Pryor or the Reverend Jessie Jackson, who once was a U.S. presidential candidate and the founder of his vision of a Rainbow Coalition.

Although my every now and then brief encounters with Raymond were positive and informative, I felt I could trust him enough to reveal to him about my past. I hadn't with other Ruth Haefner Plaza residents because I sensed they would become judgmental, turn prejudice, and not be willing to socialize. Certainly, the wrong kind of gossip would spread like an out of control forest fire. I was still in self-recovery and growing stronger each day, so I didn't need gossip to slow my pace.

I remember how I was mistreated when so-called friends and strangers saw me only as a hopeless, insufferable drunk and crack addict. One weekend while I was living with Johnny Rahwaye, Sharisse and I talked and she said that Damon had invited her to go with him and his friend Sam and Sam's girlfriend, Wanda, to a resort near Bend. Sharisse told Damon she wouldn't come unless I was invited too. In the end, Sharisse was too caught up in doing her drugs, and decided not to come, so I asked Damon if I could come with him. He reluctantly agreed, though his mood on the way to the resort was somewhat dismal; he was disappointed that Sharisse didn't come. I had told Johnny that I was going to visit my friend, Laurel, who lived in Milwaukee, Oregon, for the weekend. If I had told him otherwise – going on the trip with Damon, Johnny would no longer allow me to live with him. He had already shown me how nasty and violent he could become, especially during his intoxication.

When we got to the resort, we all went into the hot tub. Damon and I were naked, but Sam and Wanda wore swim wear. After a while, I got too hot. My heart was racing, so I got out of the hot tub before the others. After Damon exited, he walked around with just his towel around his waist. He had said that if Sharisse had come that she would've gone topless with Wanda, but Wanda never did that and neither did I. Later, we all went to eat.

Soon after our return to the resort, Damon was quick to converse with Wanda but left me out of the conversation. Sam, Wanda, and Damon were drinking their wine or cocktails. I was warned not to imbibe. However, I got upset and said to Damon, "Why won't you talk to me?" He continued to ignore me as if he was ashamed that he had asked me to come to the resort.

That night Damon had sex with me but the experience was lacking emotion on his part. It was as if he resented me being there at all, but that I was at least good for that one thing… sex at the drop of a coin. While the party of three retired, I stayed up and was sneaking drinks. I really felt left out and was sad about that, so I thought: *Why not drink?*

The next day, I sat with Damon for a long time on the couch and tried to snuggle up to him, but he wasn't interested. I put on my short skirt and see-through blouse for him. He asked me why I bothered and noticed that my clothes smelled musty from being in Johnny's storage area of his basement for too long.

I got upset again and Damon said, angrily, "I'm taking you home!" This was despite the fact that he originally planned to stay the whole weekend.

The journey back home found me seated in the back seat while Damon sat in the driver's seat. I think he preferred that arrangement because he was still angry. At one point, he accused, "You're drunk!" He screeched to a halt over to the highway median, grabbed me by the wrist and forced me out of his Jeep.

I was both stunned and pissed off over what the fool did next. He left me standing there without allowing me not to even secure my purse. Then he sped away.

My survival mode kicked in and I put my thumb out, hopefully to hitch a ride back to Portland. The weather was cold from winter; I was wearing a coat guaranteed to keep me warm, if I was not in arctic cold.

His guilty conscience must have kicked him in the balls or something because he returned to the spot where I was still thumbing for a ride.

I had intended to fight back with silence, and I did throughout our journey back to Portland. However, I had given him the look of loving eyes, of forgiveness. Too consumed with his own thoughts and driving, I don't think he sensed my caring. I did believe he resented me for being pressured to live with Johnny, and that, because of my weakness for alcohol, I would stoop so low on the food chain, and allow myself to tolerate his sexual demands. Why couldn't I just pull myself up by my own boot strings? But he never asked me that question.

I felt Damon despised me more. When he took me "home" he let me off a couple blocks away from Johnny's, like he had done when he first picked me up so that Johnny wouldn't know I had been with Damon.

Not long after that drop-off point night, I went back to soothing my various pains with steady, abusive drinking of vodka and wine. By the wee hours the next day, I was feeling crummy. I decided to go to the hospital to dry out. I asked Johnny to accompany me but he declined… telling me he cared less about me and my addiction problem.

After I arrived by ambulance to Emmanuel Hospital, I had to wait a long time for the initial intake and then they refused to hook me up to saline bags. I attempted to rise. Could I dress quick enough, then rush off? Instead, I said I would take the early morning bus home. The hospital staff prevented me from leaving, by forcing me in restraints on the unforgiving bed.

Still fighting to free myself, I shouted "Listen goddamnit. If you aren't even going to give me saline solution, I don't see why I have stay in this crummy place when I could dry out more comfortably at home!"

Perhaps thinking his leverage power wouldn't become burdensome, a marine corp type security guard grabbed my left elbow to get me under control. I must admit I wanted to use a chainsaw on their necks and present only their heads to the then current Portland City Council members at City Hall.

For me, the world stood still after I heard a distinct pop in my left elbow region. No great pain at that moment, nor throughout the night. A later and proper X-ray examination would reveal that my left elbow was broken.

The next morning, staff decided I had detoxed enough to let me go home safely. That's when I complained about my sore elbow and swelling. An X-ray came up clean. Why was that? Who authorized that to be concluded? I received pain medication and an arm slang before I exited. My pain was escalating.

Two weeks later, after more and more throbbing pain, I went to Good Samaritan Hospital. There the the staff re-examined my previous erroneous X-ray. The verdict? Absolutely *broken*. In the end, I didn't properly focus on suing.

CHAPTER TWELVE

SOLAS' FINAL DAYS AND HIS DYNAMIC REPLACEMENT

By the time I became better acquainted with Raymond during 2015, and as nationwide police brutality escalated across the country (approximately 1000 deaths), I still considered myself a lucky and successful "escapee" from acute crack cocaine and alcohol abuse. I was extra proud of myself for having defeated not only those addictions but also the defeat of what I had become: a hopeless, miserable, bottom rung loser who had attempted to kill herself. My new discipline and self-esteem enabled me to enjoy an occasional glass of wine; only one would be enough because my mind didn't consider it as pain relief medication. On the other hand, I knew that I would have to continue taking prescribed medications for the remainder of my life so I could endure fibromyalgia pain caused by the hit and run crime.

I also knew I was on the right track because I had warned my crack smoking acquaintances and friends to stop calling my cellphone number. They were hardcore pests begging me like third world refugees... wanting money to buy crack or to loan them packaged crack. They cared less that I had a significant role in my self-rehabilitation, that my will power was greater, that I was more devoted to the life and caring of my dog Solas, and that I was much wiser in handling my money. After about a dozen or more nuisance calls (one caller cussed up a storm before promising to stab me) the desperate fools quit bothering me. Oh what a relief that was, and another victory for me!

On the same day I took Solas to the vet for his annual checkup, Raymond invited me to dinner at his ground floor apartment. He especially wanted me to see his experimental collection of art objects he had crafted from used manila file folder fiber material known as *abaca*, a Spanish word.

After we ate his delicious shrimp fried rice with chunky vegetables mixed in, he just about stunned me with the history behind his self-taught process. I couldn't believe my eyes... hundreds of clever refrigerator magnets with very funny messages, beverage coasters, fashion pins, pendants, bangles, bracelets, rings, small to large 2D wall hangings, easels, salt and pepper shakers. The entire collection was breath-taking and both well-crafted and professional looking.

Sometimes even a positive first impression can fool you until you learn more facts about a newcomer in your life. Sometimes a negative first impression can have the same effect. What he revealed to me next didn't make me feel over-anxious, threatened, or becoming a victim. He had had a long history of criminal misconduct, from unarmed robberies, check forgeries, commercial burglaries to assaults. All starting after he migrated from his hometown of Richmond, Virginia. That year was 1966. A major turning point for the then eighteen year old, while the Vietnam War was on the verge of becoming more deadly, more controversial.

Not quite a mirror reflection of our back stories, but his was no less intriguing and a picture of self-destructive behaviors.

"What a crazy-ass period of my life," he said with self-reproaching disgust, after he showed me one of several pristine copies of *Oregon Home* Magazine featuring an article spotlighted on his particular creativity and medium. "If it weren't for my search for a substitute material to replace torn bits of bond typing paper in need of gluing onto a large sheet of poster board, I might have turned another 5 year prison sentence into a future life sentence without the possibility of parole."

The revelation raised my eyebrows and aroused my deeper curiosity about his background. "Incredible." I shook my head. "Why do you think that first file folder made a difference?" We we were sipping wine now, but I still hadn't revealed to him my entire history of alcohol abuse. I eventually turned down his offer of a refill.

He went on to explain the circumstances behind the felony charges: assault with a deadly weapon and attempted "technical" kidnapping of an adult female. That latter charge and conviction did raise red flags in my mind: Was I safe to be in his presence? Was he a potential rapist? Was he buttering me up with his obvious multi-talents and articulate way of expressing himself, just to catch me off guard, grab me from behind, and make me the next Caucasian victim whose throat would be slit from ear to ear? As you already know, I was mentally, physically, and sexually abused by more than a few men, several of whom were black. Maybe the non-Caucasian ones had a slight edge dishing out the destructive behaviors. The motivating factors behind his attack were three-fold: acute post release syndrome wrapped in continual denial of employment; head games with single women, and no escape from years of compulsive gambling on greyhound and thoroughbred horse racing… costing him to lose tens of thousands of dollars within a ten year period between jobs and financial gain through crime.

Out of fear and uncertainty, I could have rejected him and his back story, but I sensed he really was a good guy who expressed deep regret for his overall criminal behavior against others and business owners who became his targets. He also took full responsibility, accepted his punishments, and didn't blame The White Man for perpetrating a conspiracy to remove his black body and mind from society and deeming him a menace to society.

"Took me seventeen years, Zae, to have a change of heart and to re-steer in the right direction. I've been crime free now for over 25 years."

I couldn't help but smile as my misty eyes gazed into his attractive brown eyes. They were thirteen years older. "You did it, sir. You should be proud of all the things you've accomplished. Congratulations." We shook hands. The co-joined warmth created a tingling sensation in my palm. Possibilities of non-abusive behavior raced through my mind. Was he attracted to me? Could we mean something to each other? What would a friendship with him be like?

"Wasn't easy. Tougher than old pig skin. My freedom was challenged by a few assholes I encountered since my final release. Even now, I give *abaca* fiber much credit for opening many legitimate doors of opportunity and keeping me grounded – *regardless* of screwed-up circumstances." He finished his second glass of wine before he continued: "I saw myself becoming a professional visual artist, craftsman, and good will workshop ambassador in public schools. I wanted to show how my techniques were equated to everyday life skills needed for survival. I developed a proposal before I was paroled during spring of 1992 and presented that proposal to half a dozen Portland area middle schools."

Before my first face to face evening with him ended, I learned more about his techniques and processes and plans for the future. I couldn't have received a better dosage of inspiration. He was ambitious, visionary, and determined. The perpetuation of those qualities eventually led to his works being featured in numerous art galleries; his workshop activities in public schools, street corners, art fairs, art galleries, commercial site demonstrations, and fundraising events for non-profit organizations. Also, numerous grants and fellowships.

"I kept my promise to the parole board and I became an asset to the various communities I served," he concluded, then gave me a non-sexual hug. We were like heroic soldiers from a battlefield. In our own way, we had defeated our addiction demons for the betterment of our local society.

The following year, I invited Raymond to visit me at my Fourth Floor apartment, where there was a better collective of respectful silence among tenants than ones on other floors. We both shared a dislike for a particular notorious nuisance tenant on the Second Floor. By the time 2016 would arrive, his stack of filed complaints against that tenant would amount to over *sixty*. You'd think one or two would suffice with two replacement on-site managers and their upper management colleagues – nope. Cared less about professionally resolving the issue with at least a verbal reprimand. Didn't happen until three years later. I won't reveal all the other hectic ways Mr. Alexander went through to save his peace of mind, preventing him from committing another serious assault, or moving to another housing community for active seniors. He didn't give up on his life skills; I saw that as another victory for him. He was so serious about finding an outside remedy that he wrote an impassioned complaint letter to the newly appointed (in 2020) Portland Police Chief Chuck Lovell.

"You're welcome to stay here later," I assured him that night, "whenever that fool can't control her emotions. I get the same old crap from the resident directly below me. Doubt he has a hearing problem. Likes to hear his damn stereo thump-thump-thumping during wee hours."

For awhile, Raymond gave Solis plenty of attention with playful gestures. But at one point, Solas got his left paw entangled in the opening of a quilt spread over the couch. He couldn't free his paw after futile attempts. That's when Raymond offered to help. Instead of welcoming the assistance needed, Solas reacted by trying to bite Raymond's fingers. Solas then went on a barking rampage, his glistening, accusatory eyes as round as saucers.

After Solas calmed down and realized no threat was intended, he licked Raymond's fingers. All was forgiven by how Solas wagged his own tail.

"Ahh, man, that was a close call," he said, chuckling. "Glad I was quicker."

I replied: "I apologize for him. He loves you. He was just, you know, a little scared, like a fearful rabbit hiding in tall grass."

"No problem. I'll wear work gloves next time I visit." He was smiling.

We three resumed watching a classic movie from the 1940s.

The passage of time wasn't kind to my dear Solas. When early spring of 2017 arrived, I needed to schedule an appointment to take him to the vet because his eating habit was inconsistent and his energy level was reduced. He was still consuming medications for other ailments. His aging was a certain factor and his life expectancy for his breed – considering all other factors – was twelve to fifteen years. I prayed that the latest hurdles wouldn't take him from me permanently. I couldn't imagine it; I couldn't allow myself to dwell on it. I didn't want him to become another loyal and beloved animal friend taken from me by circumstances not under my control.

While I waited for the arrival of the appointment, I hadn't failed to ignore highlighted memories of my past, from which I showed newfound courage and determination to stay on course... no matter what hurdles I might face.

After doing door-to-door work for a couple of months, my brother got me a job doing fund-raising surveys over the phone at Gateway Communications, where he worked as Phone Room manager. I was grateful to have a regular income because my retirement money was dangerously low and I needed to pay back rent. I also walked about 4 miles total every day; to work then home. I later learned that I was going the long way around to work, but I continued my route, so I could benefit from the exercise. I started eating better and lost fifteen pounds of the weight I had previously gained.

The Phone Room was occupied by some interesting employee characters, the kind I hadn't met before. How they stayed employed would make you think that they were deep-rooted insiders possessing the darkest of company secrets, thereby affording each odd ball a You Can't Fire Me Prevention Card. I'll call one suspect "Nodding Luke". He looked like a version of a skinny kangaroo, without its characteristic ears. His clothes hung loosely on him, as if his bony frame was a clothes hanger made from Silly Putty. He was a bona fide drug user whose voice was slurred and mumbly most of the work shift. I never discovered his drug of choice.

In comparison, I nicknamed another employee. She was "Cloud Floater Maggie", around age twenty-one. She acted like she was saddled on a cumulus cloud in the sky while trying to correctly punch in her time card. Seemed like it took her a long time and great comical effort to accomplish the simple task. Maybe she was hooked on downer red pills. I've witnessed similar high-on-something conditions.

This next employee, whose hair was died a bubble gum pink, should have been awarded a tin dunce crown for emboldened stupidity. I'll call her "Loni With Too Much Free Sass". I must admit she was well-built and sexy in an exotic way. Word got around that Loni called in sick at 8:00 am and described her situation to one of our no nonsense supervisors. Loni wasn't sick... after all. Loni wasn't about to catch a bus or taxi to make up for lost time, either. Loni's excuse? *She was too busy having sex with her boyfriend. So expect to see her tomorrow morning.*

Oh no. Loni wasn't fired for telling the truth, didn't receive a scathing warning about that kind of activity not associated with her employment. I still scratch my head over that one. Some undeserving fools seem to get all the breaks.

Potential employees who were desperate for work were the ones who found work there. I, too, was desperate. I had gotten fired or let go of three previous jobs. I maintained sobriety, though, at Gateway Communications, but sometimes in the evenings I would imbibe. At one point, my previous employer, Market Strategies, wanted me back as an employee because I had done well on surveys in the past.

Encouraged and hopeful, I went there to the initial orientation on a Friday and was supposed to report to work the following Monday for training. However, I got drunk that weekend and forgot all about the training. So, I lost that job, then returned to Gateway Communications for a while. Not surprising that I would lose that job too... found "guilty" of cursing at another employee who was making too much noise talking with other co-workers, preventing me from concentrating on the duties of my job.

His real name wasn't Jeff. We had dated twice. I later discovered that he was full of deception at every turn. On our second date he told me he broke up with his psychiatrist girlfriend because she wasn't interested in having sex with him after one of her patients died. I felt like that was coldly inconsiderate because she was grieving; each of us grieve in various ways – a temporary lack of sexual interest is one.

Jeff's decayed teeth had turned yellowish brown, but I had overlooked that short-coming. My brother Bart, however, told me that Jeff was working under a fictitious name and fictitious address which turned out to be a pay–to–stay parking lot! Bart saw him often sleeping at the Portland State University Library, his makeshift home. Jeff also claimed to have a master's degree in urban studies, so why had he sought employment at Gateway Communications… considering himself being a right-wing cause advocate for funds to these organizations?

Another Gateway Communications employee was a behemoth, intimidating looking African American man whose name I don't remember. I couldn't imagine myself as a human skyscraper at 6' 7" and weighing at least 300 pounds. Fat wasn't a part of his physical equation. His cue ball shaped head was bald and glistened like a polished mahogany table top. I assumed his work experience included being a nightclub bouncer-security guard. His overall image of brutal toughness was a startling contrast to the sound of his voice: soft-spoken, almost shy… a gay prissiness suggesting to you that he wouldn't hurt a buzzing fly.

Solas demonstrated facets of his own character too. Because I deemed him as a blessing from God, I loved him deeply, unconditionally. He was like a velvety pillow cushion that would temporarily absorb the hardship pressure from my most challenging bouts of anxiety, clinical depression disorder, and PTSD. His reciprocal love gave me plenty of joy and fortified the importance of my need to continue living and thrive! The Scottish word solace means peace, as his name suggested but spelled differently.

I lacked motivation for taking beneficial daily walks. Favorite TV programs and DVD classic movies bored me to the core; even my faithful viewing of *Dark Shadows* programming had plummeted to zero. Its episodes didn't comfort me like they usually did.

The day I put Solas to sleep a crushing loneliness overwhelmed me to the point where I needed physical human comfort to help me get through the rest of that day. Excluding my family members near and far, I could count on one hand the genuine friendships I had developed at the Ruth Haefner Plaza Apartments. The only person I focused on more was my new acquaintance Raymond. I felt he would be sympathetic, understanding, and offer any kind of comfort.

The time was 3:30 pm. With tears sliding down my cheeks I punched his number on my smart phone. Took six rings before we connected.

"Hi," I said, my voice lacking enthusiasm.

"Howya doing, Zae? Sorry I didn't answer sooner." He chuckled over what he said next. "I was taking care of business in the bathroom. Going back to painting after we finish talking."

"Can you... come up and visit... for a while?" He must have sensed the anxiety in my voice.

"What's wrong?"

I didn't respond immediately.

"Zae...? What's happening? You okay?"

"I took Solas to the vet this morning."

Another reflective chuckle from him. "Did you get those crazy hair balls trimmed from his butt?"

"Not that."

"Well?"

Escalating grief caused my reluctance to answer sooner.

"I had to put him to sleep."

A seeming stunned silence from his end before he replied: *"He's gone?"*

"If you aren't busy, can you come right now?"

"Um... sure. No problem."

"I don't want to be by myself. I'll tell you what happened." His next statement was still flavored with shock and disbelief.

"But I saw him only two days ago."

"Let's talk when you get here."

I wasted no time welcoming Raymond with fresh tears streaking down my face. My body, feeling oddly feverish and weak, was trembling the moment I hugged him for morale support – like one of many ocean liner life jackets tossed in a sea of endangered passengers. The intimate tightness of the hug confirmed to me that his caring was genuine, empathetic – an older brother's compassion for a hurting little sister.

No words were spoken as we cried for what seemed like five minutes. Other long time residents, who lived at Ruth Haefner Plaza Apartments, were much more familiar with Solas than Raymond's familiarity of only nine months. That distinction didn't matter, though. His presence confirmed another truth to me: he was willing to offer his mental strength to help uplift me during my time of crisis.

Our embrace ended.

I settled on my lounge chair. Raymond settled on the adjacent sofa.

Before I began revealing why I had decided to take the alternative solution for Solas, my mind was still focused on the last minutes of his life. I wished I had been less emotionally strung out in pain and more peaceful in saying "goodbye" during the final injection, while I held him in my arms... the image of a broken mother and her fading child. I had been denied the opportunity to give birth because my ex-husband, before I met him, had had a vasectomy.

I became more crushed when I saw the final light of inner life vanish minute by minute from his eyes. Somehow, his weakened condition allowed him to twist his head just right. He then bit the thumb of my right hand but no blood escaped. Was that his way of telling me I had betrayed the love we had established over a decade ago? As I write to conclude that heart-breaking moment, I can't avoid crying. A colorful metal container holds his precious ashes in the living room.

"Solas was twelve and a half years old. He suffered from liver and arthritis problems. I swear, Raymond, I was clueless that he was suffering from *diabetes!*" I couldn't hold back more crying. "I got that diagnosis six months after the liver diagnosis. Maybe that also contributed to his screwed up eating habits and mood swings." I rose, hurried to the kitchen, snatched a paper towel sheet, then returned to the living room. I cleared my congested nose.

"I didn't know dogs could get diabetes," Raymond said. "I have human friends dealing with that problem."

"The vet told me I would have to give Solas an insulin shot everyday for the rest of his life."

Raymond shook his head, no less sympathetic. "He wouldn't have liked that routine. At times, he bit you for trying to help him."

"That's what I feared most: his complete rejection of injected life-saving medicine." I cleared my nose again. "Wouldn't have mattered if I were the gentlest nurse in the world. A needle puncture everyday wasn't for him."

Silence washed over us for a moment.

I was gazing at a framed photo of my Solas propped on the shoulder of my of apartment's large rectangular window. Position of a 4:00 pm sun illuminated his Maltipoo breed face and intelligent blue eyes. Sweet memories of him bounced around in my mind like runaway ping pong balls. I went so deep in to the past that otherwise annoying sounds of speeding Beaverton-Hillsdale Highway rush hour traffic didn't bother me. I already knew that finding a replacement animal friend was going to be difficult because I was so deeply attached to him. I was his devoted surrogate mother for almost thirteen years. Sure, there were some not fun times but they didn't overshadow the hilarious and loving times.

"Your veterinarian offered no other treatment for Solas?" Raymond said, after he returned with two goblets of white wine.

"Nothing, damnit. I didn't want to torture him everyday with an insuline shot."

"Right. I wouldn't like it, either. My good friend Marsha – she's a visual artist and crafter, pokes herself at least twice a day." He shook his head before he took another sip. "Too much for me, Zae."

"Without immediate insuline treatment, the vet warned me Solas would live only two weeks."

Raymond slapped his thigh. "Oh shit!"

"This is what pissed me off: he seemed unwilling to give me enough time to think about the situation – a *rush* job."

"At least an hour."

" The next day would've worked better."

"I would have, if I were him. I hope he didn't dislike you for whatever reason. Who knows for sure."

I took a sip. "Well screw him. I feel so damn guilty; maybe I'll feel that way until I die."

"You had mercy in mind, Zae. You shouldn't bang your head against a brick wall for sparing Solas more trauma. The other alternative would've been hellish for both of you. Tearing you apart, emotionally and physically."

The way Raymond used practical common sense thinking inspired me to believe I made the right choice for my beloved Solas. My deep mixed emotions persisted, though.

After Raymond left to return to his apartment, he phoned me the next day for a welfare check. He asked how I was feeling. I told him grief wasn't an easy condition that could be swept under a rug and be forgotten. I told him I needed another dog in my life because Solas and I had rescued each other and our bonding was almost instant. Raymond suggested I avoid thinking about searching for a replacement too soon and allow my grief to subside, thereby giving me the opportunity to regain my emotional strength. My resistance against his suggestion boosted my self-confidence.

After nearly two more months of grieving, coupled with depression and anxiety, I decided to conduct an Internet search. Solas' framed photos mounted here and there (plus bulging photo albums!) was a daily reminder of the hairy white treasure I had loss. I thought another Maltipoo, but a so-called teacup one, would be a therapeutic blessing and easier to deal with since I was well acquainted with the breed. Of course, I wasn't going to allow that factor to deter me from selecting a different breed. However, I preferred a low maintenance, stable-minded, medium-size dog that needed to be rescued from a shelter.

June of 2020 finally arrived. The Covid-19 virus was spreading nationwide – killing thousands of citizens each day, and becoming a stronger, nastier pandemic. I, too, wore masks like a faithful member of a cult. I'm still so thankful to God for helping to protect me, my family members, Phyllis, Raymond, and other true friends. None of us were infected.

Excited about finding another dog friend, my preliminary internet search targeted the website of the Oregon Humane Society in Portland and the website of the Oregon Dog Rescue in the city of Tualatin. The first non-profit didn't have the breed of dog I felt comfortable adopting; the second non-profit had a better selection. I wrote down a few interesting names and breed descriptions that captured my imagination and uplifted my hope. Shortly thereafter, I made an appointment to visit the facility. My friend Louise took me there in her car.

In 2007, Oregon Dog Rescue was founded by Deb Bowen and Krystyna Schmidt. Able to accommodate up to 75 dogs, it is a no-kill shelter serving the greater Portland area. Deb and Krystyna have a combined twelve years of experience rescuing dogs and devoted to placing them in the best homes and assuring the long-term success of adoptions. Their four-legged clients come from overcrowded local shelters, owners who can no longer keep their dogs, and from high-kill shelters in the following states: California, Texas, Mexico, Washington and Oregon. (Note: this non-profit is moving in late 2023/early 2024, to a larger facility on South Macadam Avenue in Portland, Oregon.)

A petite, red-haired staff member greeted me and Louise at the service counter while dog clients provided a cacophony of enthusiastic barking in a brightly illuminated rear section of the facility. Several volunteers were busy with duties in the spacious lobby area.

My heart raced as if I were exercising on a trade mill. Rivulets of sweat tickled my itchy lower back. My palms grew moist from more nervous energy and anticipation. This situation was no less a mystery in need of being solved before midnight. I tried my best not to show repeat swallowing of reduced saliva production. A male's bobbing Adam apple would have exposed my predicament. I almost stuttered my introduction. "I'm Zae Rankin. I have a 2 pm appointment. Adoption consideration."

"Oh wonderful! I'm Wilma." Her smile was toothy, bright. "Thank you for coming, ma'am."

"This is my friend Louise. My ride. She's not here to adopt."

"Fine. Welcome, Louise."

"Hi." Louise was more preoccupied with gazing at wall mounted posters of ridiculously cute puppies of various breeds in playful modes and wanting to melt your heart with unconditional love and affection – *yes yes yes!*

We followed perky Wilma along a hallway leading to an entrance with a security door with an observation window. The cacophony of barking gave me goose bumps. My anticipation and excitement further escalated. I had scheduled an hour to look at and to consider the two candidates I selected from the website.

"Here we are," Wilma announced. "As you can see, our dogs are friendly, well behaved, and waiting to lick your face till the cows wander back home."

We laughed.

I scanned the reasonably clean cubicles as we followed Wilma to the section of cubicles where my potential candidates were housed. The first one's name was Allison, even a popular name for human females.

Immediately, my heart reached out to the dear-headed, cream colored canine that gave me the impression of a scared and trembling hamster. I was told she was a larger Chihuahua mix breed; shy of new people and new situations she would face. I thought she looked downright innocent, a pitiful specimen standing in the corner of her neat cubicle, her tail tucked between her legs, one ear in normal position, the other easily floppy. Her bold, glistening dark eyes stared at me the entire time.

I groaned as I lowered to my knees but I didn't dare remain in that position too long because of past knee surgery. "Allison..." I waited about twenty seconds. I then attempted a soothing, everything is gonna be alright tone. "Allison... come here, honey. I like you very much. Okay? I want to be your best mommie. Let me love you."

"Here. Give her this tasty treat," Wilma said. "Afterward, you can enter."

I managed to toss the pebble within several feet from her front legs. A shock of satisfaction went through my heart when she took timid, unsure steps toward the waiting offering.

Louise said to me, "As quickly as possible, you need to form a bond with her – just *you*, okay?"

"You bet." Each time I called out her name and she gave me her undivided attention, I clicked the clicker I had brought with me. Her smartness allowed her to catch on sooner than I expected. She associated the meaning behind the clicking sound with receiving a treat of cheese or hot dog round.

Oh thank god! Allison summoned enough courage to come to me and secure the second treat from my palm. That was my cue to sit on the floor. I watched her munch in seeming delight. After that thrilling development, I knew beyond all doubt that I wanted to love, cherish, and protect Allison. I ached to pet her, ached to reassure her of my commitment and dedication.

She had just been spaded a week before and her stitches were out and I learned that she originally came from California and had a litter of puppies and then had been with a foster mom for awhile before she was transferred to the Oregon Dog Rescue facility. I thought how sad that she no longer had a home, after just two years of her life, except for the dog rescue non-profit.

The staff there informed me that Allison's foster mom was going to swing by, but she never did. Also, Allison became withdrawn and built a self-protective demeanor after her transition to the facility. I figured she would become a one-person companion, hopefully bonding mostly with me in my particular environment. However, a single bonding could present problems in the future. Think of young married couples who want time for themselves away from home... go out to a movie or a restaurant but have trouble finding the right babysitter when trustworthy relatives aren't available to assist them. They have no other alternative, and so they must remain at home.

In Louise's car I held Allison in my lap. A rhythmic, low tempo Bossa Nova tune of Brazillian origins was playing on the radio. With tender strokes of my hand working her head and upper neck regions, I wanted her to trust me while trying to quell her trembling.

"I think she's gonna turn out be a sweet, loving companion down the road," Louise said, smiling.

"I sure hope so," I said. "Bonding takes time. I have enough patience." Allison started whimpering. "Solas taught me about having patience."

I wasted no time getting my adoptee familiar with the backyard of Ruth Haefner Plaza Apartments, where she wasted no time relieving herself. The grounds, having large shade trees, grassy areas, and seating arrangements, was spacious enough to accommodate the presence of numerous residents and their canine companions. (A few cats were residents but they were mostly homebound trained. They would make rare appearances in the hallways and rocket away back to safety when they saw you approaching.)

When Allison was about to shut down again and desiring not to move an inch, I lifted her up and carried her to the lobby where one of two elevators would take us to the Fourth Floor where I lived.

I then spent a couple of hours watching TV while I held her in my arms. In spite of my fingers stroking gently, the rigidity of her body made me feel her loneliness. My whispery tone said to her, "This is your forever home, honey. Just like it was Solas'. He was sweet and obedient for many years. Unless I'm hospitalized, I will never abandon you because you're extra special." On that first day of bonding, I was hoping she would feel and be soothed by my affection.

The Oregon Dog Rescue staff had warmed me that Allison was a flight risk, so I bought a special safety collar designed to tighten if she tried to get loose from it. Only yards away was situated four lanes of vehicular traffic with a posted speed limit of 45; some impatient motorists dared to go 60. A *significant* danger zone for both inattentive pedestrians and unleashed canines. Squirrels, crows, pigeons, and sparrows were usually the death statistics. The staff also told me that she probably wouldn't eat for the first couple of days in a new place. I was given a small supply of dry and wet food she had been used to eating at the facility. To my surprise, she ate like a starved wolf in the wild that first night, as if my apartment already was very familiar to her.

"It's bedtime, Allison," I said to her. Without much hesitation she followed me to the bedroom – happily wagging her tail – and jumped up onto the bed. We snuggled. We fell asleep.

I suppose the dream happened during the wee hours of the next day. I can't recall how it ended...

In cinematic slow motion my rescuer Solas was running in the dog park. The air was perfumed by the scents of wild flowers and thriving grass. We were alone, except for early morning song birds chirping like contest competitors in a volley ball match. Each time I threw his favorite squeaky toy a longer distance he chased it, shook it, and returned it to me. On his own he rolled over onto his back so I could massage his belly region. He was enjoying the affection he was accustomed to receiving from me. Afterward, he licked my tear-stained face, as if his tongue was a washcloth, as if this gesture would foreshadow our future....

Those first few days were spent training Allison to come take a treat from me when I called her name. I trained her to get used to the double set of mechanical doors separating the lobby perimeter from the foyer perimeter housing a resident call unit. There were times when I still had to carry her out when the doors opened to the outside and leading to the backyard.

After about a week of more in-house training I took her on her first journey along the sidewalk of Beaverton-Hillsdale Highway. I also began feeding her in her carrier which I propped up on the top of my personal folding grocery cart, whenever I needed to do shopping at nearby stores. I got her used to being around shoppers. Somehow, she understood that her carrier meant it was a temporary safe haven.

Eventually, I took her to the grocery store just on her leash. We walked inside. I purchased my daily lemon parfait, did business at the pharmacy, and waited in the checkout line. Throughout all that activity my little princess Allison didn't complain. So far, I was proud of her cooperative attitude. However, she had a tendency to shake in apprehension whenever we journeyed downstairs in one of two elevators. She would bark at all strangers around her; to a lesser extent bark at familiar people. Gradually, she stopped shaking.

It was during a dinner date at my apartment when I introduced her to my new friend Raymond. She was turning out to be a good alert dog because his door knocking triggered her protective barking. It continued until he settled on the couch.

"Solas' dynamic replacement, huh?" Raymond said. He didn't seem intimidated by her riotous barking and defensive stance. "Oh man. A real firecracker." She didn't lunge to bite him but she resisted his attempt to pet her while I held her in my arms. I provided some details of her background. He shook his head. "Too bad about her puppies… stolen from her. I know you would have loved seeing them."

"I hope each one looks like her and placed in a loving home."

After we finished eating, we watched movies. I suggested he give her a before-bedtime-treat. She refused the offering; she wouldn't accept treats from anyone else's hand yet.

We got more conversational.

Raymond revealed his experiences with canine and feline pet companions, while as a teen living in Richmond, Virginia and after he migrated to Portland, Oregon. Years later, he lived with a girlfriend in a rent-to-buy house with a postage stamp size backyard lacking a fence. On his 22nd birthday she gave him a pure bred German shepherd puppy that was bigger than normal. Coming up with a catchy name was a challenge. After some brainstorming, he decided to call the puppy Black Sabbath.

By the time he was six months old, he stood a monstrous five feet tall and weighed at least 75 pounds.

Raymond wasn't familiar with the dynamics of separation anxiety in unconditioned pet companions. He and his girlfriend wanted to go out to dinner then dance at a popular night club. They figured they'd be gone for at least four hours. They provided Black Sabbath with plenty of food, water, rigorous hugs, and "I love yous".

Then they exited.

They returned around midnight, not expecting a disaster.

What they saw was stunning and disappointing. Each accent pillow that graced the couch was now ripped apart and its stuffings spilled like confetti. Separation anxiety had triggered Black Sabbath's anger and he also expressed it by crapping and urinating multiple times. Pillow stuffings even littered the kitchen *and* bathroom. Coffee table mounted magazines were shredded. The upstairs bedroom wasn't spared the violence. Crap and urine on the carpet. Pillows ripped apart and stuffings scattered. An end table lamp toppled and cracked.

The entire motif of violence triggered anger especially in Raymond. He told me he didn't want to physically punish the German shepherd but it happened. He didn't believe in animal cruelty and he wasn't too merciless. His birthday present learned a lesson too.

I also found out that Allison had separation anxiety because my assigned Russian housekeeper said Allison would whine and bark the whole time in her carrier while I was absent – walking, for example, to and from Albertson's Supermarket. One time I was absent from her for almost an hour. My housekeeper's report that time wasn't positive.

I consulted with a local trainer and she told me that I would have to start with being away from her for five seconds and gradually work up to minutes, etc., etc.

Over a period of a year, Allison got used to Raymond's occasional presence in my apartment. We shared discussions about numerous topics: abstract art, crafting, classic movies from the 40s, 50s, 60s, books we've read, places we've been, race relations, the economy, and past intimate relationships.

Passage of time allowed Allison to start bonding with him. He taught her how to do a high-five gesture, without him having to entice her with her favorite doggy treat. She also started bonding with my next-door-neighbor Phyllis who had medical issues and required the assistance of an electric wheelchair. Phyllis was like a surrogate grandmother who was generous with her own style of love and affection. An unabashed spoiler with doggy treats and doggy gifts. She herself is the proud parent of a bearded dragon species she named Walter. I kid you not. He is an avid TV watcher preferring movement of animated animals! His diet (yikes!) consists of commercially grown roaches and plump worms. Other residents scatter for safety, fearing him whenever Phyllis has him propped on her shoulder, as she travels in her electric wheelchair along the stretch of lobby or parks in the extended day room area.

Caroline, another reliable and consistent friend, is the owner of canine companion Rocky – a package of energetic friendliness. He's a so-called "Chiweenie" (a mixture of Chihuahua and Dachshund). His smooth coat is tobacco-like brown with charcoal black streaks. He and Allison needed no coaxing introduction to become instant friends on their first meeting... tail wagging, nose nudging, and rear end sniffing signaling good vibrations and genuine chemistry.

The rambunctious duo would spend each day of the summer months running and playing together in the back yard. Later, during the winter of 2022, Allison became better acquainted with Phyllis. She had been a long time friend to my departed Solas. Likewise, Phyllis reached out to Allison by opening her home to her every day, letting her explore floor-based property and various smells of interest to her nose – without approaching her – just giving her the freedom to explore until she advanced toward Phyllis fingering a delicious treat.

Several months later, Allison and Phyllis became the best of friends, and, according to Phyllis' mind set, "our" little dog jumps into her lap and takes treats from her every day.

My adoptee Allison has learned to become comical. For no apparent reason, she likes to race from lounging on the bedroom bed to doing a flying squirrel leap onto the living room couch. Although not good for her health but perhaps a delight to her taste buds, I have to stop her from chewing cardboard scraps she manages to sneak into her cozy round mobile bed in the living room. She likes a little macho play with Raymond, giving him "love bites" to his fingers during wrestling matches. Her behavior, whenever she sits on a makeshift throne of couch pillows, is somewhat a mystery to me. I have no deep knowledge of dog psychology, but why would a female dog hump a favorite cylindrical pillow made of super-strong fabric? The aggressive biting and humping routine, having started in early 2022, should be more associated with male dog desire. One thing for sure, several minutes of that kind of workout quickly drains her of energy.

She loves her variety of squeaky toys and sectioned feeding bowl enhanced with smart technology that plays (whenever her paw manages to open a closed pocket concealing pebbly treats) several tunes and lights up in different colors. She would make an excellent commercial ambassador of chewing on so-called bully sticks made of collagen. They resemble large bones and can last her for several days. She also loves her good weather walks with me. She seems afraid of large dogs she encounters. Otherwise, she will approach and say hello to most little dogs, ones not residing at Ruth Haefner.

Lastly, I remain thankful to God for having given me my life back, even though I take some credit for the duration of my self-rehabilitation and defeat of crack cocaine and alcohol abuse. I thank Him for giving me the passion and strength to love those animals – the pigs, the goats and lambs, the dogs, the chickens – that crossed my path, especially at my grandparents Double Eagle Farm in the vicinity of Vale, Oregon. We loved each other deeply. I still miss their presence and their teachings during my childhood. I am thankful for having a strong-willed brother (love you madly, Bart; I salute you for your efforts and standing tall while facing your own challenges!) whose monumental patience and tough love helped me to survive during my darkest days and when rejection by so-called acquaintances and friends (addicted dangerous ones included) turned into threats against my life. My parents, perhaps thinking it was wise of them to not give up on me, deserve credit for helping to keep me buoyed during the many ridiculous housing transitions I had created because of my addictions and unwillingness to conquer them much sooner. My parents gave me the empathy gene and I faithfully applied it from an early age to loving animals and nature.

Here's a poem dedicated to those of you who are, especially so, animal companion parent(s) living with you, protecting you, being an ongoing and invaluable asset in your life:

> Dogs and cats – not excluding other lovable creatures
> as gifts to the world – are like valuable spices offering
> pleasure to your mind and big heart... uncomplicated
> smaller creatures you cherish each and every day.
>
> Perhaps you made sacrifices – time, money, patience, a
> change of priorities – before your scheduled visit to either
> a local shelter or out-of-state one harboring a needy furry
> breed... eagerly waiting to bring a recipe of happiness and
> peace into your human world.
>
> Perhaps maximum age longevity claimed your best animal
> companion that played an integral role in you and your
> family's existence. Perhaps a shelter candidate was taken to
> your home to provide companionship to another animal
> companion that has contributed selfless love, abundance of
> affection, and provided protection against the nastiness of
> foolish strangers bent on destruction.

Seeking Solace

I salute you for your humanitarianism, thus allowing their precious lives to shine brighter than heavenly stars. Without you and other empathetic citizens like you not being there for them would surely create a devastating world of indifference, coldness, and sadness. And that, dear owners, would be a waste of domesticated animal magnetism.

EPILOGUE

TEN COLLABORATOR QUESTIONS

1. *Have you learned additional lessons about your life's journey?*
   ZAE: I have learned that it is never too late or hopeless to find yourself in a better emotional state – being happy is a *choice*. Life throws us scary obstacles or in my case, addictions and health issues which, ultimately, could have been the end of me. There is hope, love, and peace in simple things. In my case, I considered animals as my children and each one played an important part of my journey. Overall, they helped my mental health and showed me the power of unconditional love... being priceless in its offering. I, too, have learned to empathize and to love beyond myself with the help of friends, relatives, and animals. Furthermore, I've learned that perseverance and seeking help (not to be ashamed of) when needed are essential for my well-being.

2. *At any point, did the "horror" stories of other alcohol/drug abusers create in you a self-imposed deterrent?*
   ZAE: When I often went to AA or NA meetings I would feel an affinity for others struggling with these same problems, but I stopped going because I would often feel like drinking/using again after hearing these stories. The confessional healing technique wasn't much of a deterrent for me. I was too overpowered by hopelessness and a need to self-destruct. I didn't know how to deal with loss or pain until I went

through it myself the hard way. I had had enough of both, recognizing that the addictions were causing my unhappiness.

3. **What role did your family play in helping you to stay focused when your addictions became less a complexity and burden?**

    ZAE: My mom went to Al-Anon (a non-profit organization dedicated to having family members assist in group sessions with an addicted family member). As was mentioned before, she paid my rent when I was having a hard time finding a job that would pay enough to cover my expenses. Her grateful assistance was predicated on me staying clean and sober for the rest of my life. She was my selfless angel of mercy when I needed her most.

4. **How many times had you contemplated suicide and carried out attempts?**

    ZAE: I contemplated suicide on a few occasions after the depressive effect of drinking too much alcohol that always hit me like repetitive punches from a boxing glove. One time, when I was literally penniless, my desperation was so acute that I consumed rubbing alcohol! That horrible experience landed me in the hospital. I could have died from poisoning that day. Maybe blinded me. Maybe torched my brain and made it useless.

5. **What was your lowest point of profound misery, before seriously focusing on either rehabilitation or self-rehabilitation?**

    ZAE: The answer to question #4 would most definitely qualify as one of three lowest points.

6. **Were you motivated, while under the influence of chemicals, to avoid nonviolent crimes that could have you hauled to prison? Or did you care less about consequences?**

    ZAE: I wasn't motivated enough to even think about committing a non-violent crime, unlike tens of thousands of potential criminals do everyday in America. I guess I was lucky or just too scared of the consequences: jail or prison time, loss of freedom and rights associated with it.

7. *What was your campaign toward self-rehabilitation and do you advise other addicted personalities to pursue that goal?*

ZAE: I talked with my primary care doctor and a psychiatrist about my chronic and severe physical and mental pain. Both doctors came up with a variety of medications which helped me so much. This concoction took a while to manifest in my system, though. A trial and error approach. I explained to them that, through my own "cold turkey" self-rehabilitation efforts, I defeated my addictions. I also prayed a lot. I can't advise other addicts to carryout the particular way I championed for myself, to save myself. Just don't be afraid of professional help if you feel self-rehabilitation is too much of a hurdle, a brick wall that you think you can't penetrate and knock down.

8. *How long have you been non-alcohol dependent?*

ZAE: 17 years… knock wood. I must congratulate my loving self.

9. *Do you feel you're strong and wise enough to battle against even the lightest motivation to abuse alcohol again?*

ZAE: Yes. I'm not addicted anymore. Nowadays, I'm only a very light, *unpressured* drinker: about one glass of wine every week – if I'm in the mood.

10. *What final advice do you have to offer readers and others trapped in a cage of alcohol and drug addiction?*

ZAE: Don't give up on yourself. Life is so much more worthwhile when you are no longer trapped in this cage. Focus on the wonderful little things in life that gives you pleasurable organic rewards (don't ever discount real love for temporary sexual lust). A closer interaction with relatives and friends (including dogs and cats and other domesticated ones) can help keep you on track.

THE END

Printed in the USA
CPSIA information can be obtained
at www.ICGtesting.com
LVHW041232051023
760079LV00002B/476